W9-BYK-794

THE
ISIS
CRISIS

CHARLES H. DYER AND MARK TOBEY

MOODY PUBLISHERS

CHICAGO

All Scripture quotations, unless otherwise indicated, are taken from the *New American Standard Bible*®, Copyright © 1960, 1962, 1963, 1968, 1971, 1972, 1973, 1975, 1977, 1995 by The Lockman Foundation. Used by permission. (www.Lockman.org)

Scripture quotations marked nkjv are taken from the New King James Version. Copyright © 1982 by Thomas Nelson, Inc. Used by permission. All rights reserved.

Scripture quotations marked niv are taken from the Holy Bible, New International Version®, NIV®. Copyright © 1973, 1978, 1984, 2011 by Biblica, Inc.™ Used by permission of Zondervan. All rights reserved worldwide. www.zondervan.com. The "NIV" and "New International Version" are trademarks registered in the United States Patent and Trademark Office by Biblica, Inc.™

Photographs in chapter 7 are courtesy of Charles Dyer, the author.

Edited by Jim Vincent
Interior and cover design: Erik M. Peterson
Cover image of militant copyright © 2013 by zabelin/iStock. All rights reserved.

All websites listed herein are accurate at the time of publication, but may change in the future or cease to exist. The listing of website references and resources does not imply publisher endorsement of the site's entire contents.

Library of Congress Cataloging-in-Publication Data

Dyer, Charles H.
The ISIS crisis : what you really need to know / Charles H. Dyer, Mark Tobey.
    pages cm
Includes bibliographical references.
ISBN 978-0-8024-1318-5
1. IS (Organization) 2. Terrorism—Religious aspects—Islam. 3. Terrorism—Iraq—History. 4. Terrorism—Middle East—History. 5. Islamic fundamentalism—History. 6. Middle East—History—21st century. I. Title.
HV6433.I722D94 2015
261.2'7--dc23
                    2014046448

We hope you enjoy this book from Moody Publishers. Our goal is to provide high-quality, thought-provoking books and products that connect truth to your real needs and challenges. For more information on other books and products written and produced from a biblical perspective, go to www.moodypublishers.com or write to:

Moody Publishers
820 N. LaSalle Boulevard
Chicago, IL 60610

3 5 7 9 10 8 6 4 2

Printed in the United States of America

This book is lovingly dedicated to the men and women proclaiming the gospel on the front lines of ministry across the Middle East.

"And they overcame him because of the blood of the Lamb and because of the word of their testimony, and they did not love their life even when faced with death."
REVELATION 12:11

CONTENTS

FOREWORD

T he international terror group known as ISIS has been grabbing headlines in the past few months, and the book you hold in your hands is critical for understanding ISIS and its role in the future of the Middle East.

Charles Dyer and Mark Tobey have done a great service in helping us see that ISIS did not arise in a vacuum but is actually part of a larger tapestry of Middle East history, religion, and politics. In these pages, you will learn how the decisions made by the Allies after World War I helped shape the context for today's conflict and unrest. At that time, with the defeat of Turkey plunging the Ottoman Empire into disarray, the British, French, and Russians decided to divide up much of the crumbling empire for themselves—helping set the stage for the conflicts we see today.

There are several reasons why you should read this book.

First, you will be introduced to the complexity of the Middle East. You will learn the differences between Shiites and Sunnis, and between the Ottomans, the Assyrians, and the Kurds. You will learn how the 1979 Russian invasion of Afghanistan galvanized a group of fighters who would eventually develop into the radical Islamic terrorist organizations that have gained both wealth and fearsome power. In addition, you will be given a basic primer on Islam, the religion that weaves its way throughout the convoluted history of the Middle East. Islam condemns democracy and views the West as being ruled by decadent imperialists who use their superior power to exploit those regions of the world that cannot resist them.

You will learn that President Obama misspoke when he said that ISIS is not Islamic. At its core, Islam is a political religion that seeks to dominate the world. Terror groups, citing Quranic commands to rid the world of all infidels, desire an ideal Islamic state that would encompass the world. As we know, these groups have America in their long-term sights.

A second reason to read this book is to better understand Israel, a country and a people spurned by the surrounding nations and the wider Islamic world. A superficial understanding of the Middle East might lead one to believe that this rejection was caused by the birth of the Israeli state in 1948, which displaced many Arabs to other territories, such as the West Bank. However, Islamic hatred for the Jews dates from a much earlier time, back to the prophet Muhammad, who oversaw the beheading of seven hundred Jewish men; he then enslaved their wives and children. This book points out the violent statements and commands found in the Quran that fuel rage against the Jews. This explains why ISIS uses these direct statements from the Quran and the Hadith to justify its brutality against all perceived infidels, whether Jewish, Christian, or even Islamic.

The third and most important reason to read this book is that all of these events are discussed against the background of the Scriptures. Although the authors do not believe that the Antichrist will arise out of the Islamic religion, we are treated to a general framework of Middle East prophecy. No surprise to us, it is clear that in the end, Jesus wins! ISIS represents a crisis for us, but not for the One who will be declared King of kings and Lord of lords.

This is a serious book, one you will want to read more than

once. Read it the first time to grasp the general flow of Middle East history; then, like me, you will want to read it a second time in more detail, to unravel the nuances and various players in the Middle East and to come to grips with the terror groups that threaten our security.

After reading this book, I promise you will never see the Middle East in the same way again. You will move beyond our sound-bite culture and realize that while Middle Eastern history is multifaceted and often confusing, it also yields its lessons to those who are willing to learn.

ERWIN W. LUTZER
Senior pastor, The Moody Church, Chicago
Bestselling author

INTRODUCTION: ISIS ON THE MOVE

*If you see the Black Banners coming from Khurasan,
go to them immediately, even if you must crawl over ice,
because indeed amongst them is the Caliph, Al Mahdi.*

Then from the direction of the East will emerge black flags.

FROM THE HADITH

In a small town in northern Iraq, villagers shield their eyes from the setting sun as they gaze toward the horizon. The lengthening shadows and the golden hue of the impending sunset add depth and color to the stark brown-and-white canvas of Iraq's arid terrain.

But the villagers aren't outside admiring the sinking sun. Instead, they stare anxiously at an ominous column of dust rising in the distance. The cloudless sky and calm wind don't suggest an approaching storm. And yet, a tempest of a far more serious kind is brewing that will soon wreak havoc on everyone in its path.

As the column of dust draws closer, the source becomes clear. Speeding down the dirt road toward town are an odd assortment of Humvees, pickup trucks, and SUVs packed with men carrying rifles and automatic weapons. Affixed to poles held high by the masked warriors are black flags snapping in the hot desert air. On each flag, in flowing Arabic, are the words of the *Shahada*, "There is no God but Allah, Muhammad is the messenger of Allah." At the bottom of the flag is the seal of Muhammad.

This is the Black Banner, or Black Standard. Unlike the Jolly Roger flown from the masts of pirate ships in a Robert Louis Stevenson story, the Black Banner is no fanciful metaphor of high seas adventure. The Black Flag is real. It is very real. And it is intended to strike terror in all who see it—to make a very specific statement about the group's aim and intent. They've come to hunt, capture, torture, and kill, without mercy.

The Black Flag symbolizes militant Islam on the move. It represents the Islamic State advancing to swallow and control still another village, all the while terrorizing all who live there. It even points to the end of days and the arrival of the *Mahdi* . . . Islam's promised Messiah.

ISIS is on the move.

WHILE WE WERE SLEEPING

In the beginning this new group of Islamic Jihadists received little attention from the West. For the last twenty years or more, Americans and many other Western countries have been sleeping through the night of evil's emerging fury. Yet in that time the stage has become ideal for the unleashing of a level of extremism and violent aggression not witnessed since Hitler's assault on the Jews in Europe.

Iraq, it seems, is only the trailhead of a much larger path, down which ISIS is determined to march. More recently, over thirty-seven different rebel factions have been fighting against Bashar al-Assad, president of Syria, and the Syrian Army. The

Free Syrian Army and the Al-Nusra Front are the largest, and they have received all the press coverage and outside funds.

At first, this new group, calling itself ISIS—the Islamic State in Iraq and Syria—appeared to be one of several Al-Qaeda-affiliated groups engaged in the fight. Basically, nothing to worry about in the wider context of the Middle East conflict. In an interview for the *New Yorker* magazine in early 2014, President Barak Obama, hoping to reassure the world, referred to ISIS as a "jayvee team."[1]

We all rolled over and went back to sleep.

A NIGHTMARE UNFOLDS

In less than nine months, however, President Obama's so-called JV team has vaulted to the front page with three headline-grabbing moves. First, they bested Syrian and Iraqi forces in battle and captured a large swath of territory, including Mosul, Iraq's second largest city. Next, after sweeping into Mosul, they declared the land captured to be an Islamic state—a *caliphate*. Their goal is to expand that state until the Black Flag flies boldly across the entire Middle East. Finally, ISIS shocked the world by brutally beheading "infidels" in the land they had conquered, including Christians, women and children, and members of other religious minorities unwilling to convert, along with Western reporters and aid workers captured during their violent campaigns.

That's when we all finally woke up. ISIS isn't just a bad dream. It's is a real-life nightmare unfolding before our eyes.

This supposed JV team suddenly was defeating all rivals in what seemed like an almost unstoppable drive to dominate the Middle East. Soon President Obama recognized the terrorist military group as a major threat. He gave them a slightly different name: ISIL, for the Islamic State of Iraq and the Levant. ("Levant" is an early geographical term referring to the land between Egypt and Turkey, which today includes Syria, Lebanon, Jordan, and Israel.)[2]

The rapid rise of ISIS raises a series of questions:

- Where did ISIS come from?
- Why did its sudden rise take everyone by surprise?
- Are ISIS leaders and soldiers really a serious threat to the Middle East? Do they have the ability to attack Europe and America?
- Can they be stopped? If so, how?
- Does the rise of this "Islamic State" have any biblical significance?
- Is the "ISIS Crisis" little more than a blip on an already-cluttered Middle East radar or could they indeed be pushing the world toward Armageddon?
- How can we remain calm as the world is seemingly coming unglued?
- How can we respond in ways that make sense and are rational and even compassionate, when fear seems easily to overwhelm us?

This book will help answer those questions for you.

Nothing happens without a cause. In other words, to understand the future we must peer into the past. Turns out, recent history will help us understand how ISIS so quickly found its place in our sleepy and comfortable civilized world —a world that apparently continually forgets how history without discretion, and at times with an almost courageous resolve, insists on repeating itself.

1

THE WAR TO END WAR

Those who cannot remember the past are condemned to repeat it.

GEORGE SANTAYANA
Spanish Philosopher[1]

After the release of a video showing the beheading of journalist James Foley in August 2014, President Barak Obama stood before the nation and declared, "One thing we can all agree on is that a group like ISIL has no place in the twenty-first century."[2]

President Obama expressed our collective rage and horror over this brutal execution of a Western hostage by an ISIS soldier. And yes, we all agreed: ISIS must be stopped.

Yet, since then, there have been more beheadings. Shocking reports of children and women being brutalized and murdered at the hands of these terrorists have rattled even the most apathetic among us. Reports on nightly newscasts have chronicled confusing details of ISIS gaining more and more control over key regions of the Middle East. How can something like this be happening in such a civilized, highly sophisticated world?

As strong as President Obama's words may have been at the time, they did not answer all our questions . . . or calm all our fears. What's more, the media's attempt to make sense of it all leaves most people dazed and bewildered. And our questions go unanswered. Where in the world did a group like this come from? And how can they be stopped?

ISIS has threatened to send its soldiers to attack the United Kingdom, the United States, and other countries. When will they make their way into my neighborhood? Are they already here?

Fear feeds off lack of understanding and an ignorance of the truth. That's why it's so important for everyone to understand the origin and motives behind ISIS and to be best prepared for a very uncertain future.

HOW IT ALL BEGAN

To understand the rise of ISIS, we need to travel back in time a hundred years. Our journey takes us to Europe in the dark days of World War I, the "war to end war."[3] Events from the front lines dominated the news, but political intrigue and shifting alliances slinked through the power corridors of London, Paris, and Moscow. Treaties and secret agreements were forged that unknowingly created problems that would cripple the Middle East for the next hundred years . . . and led to the rise of ISIS.

World War I pitted the Allied Powers (Great Britain, France, Russia, and later the United States) against the Central Powers (Germany, Austria-Hungary, and the Ottoman Empire). The conflict centered in Europe and quickly degenerated into a brutal war of attrition that ultimately claimed the lives of nine million soldiers and seven million civilians.

Advances in technology multiplied the number of dead and wounded as each side developed more efficient and effective weapons, including submarines, airplanes, and poison gas.

The Allied powers needed to find a way to break the stalemate in the trenches of Europe. Their solution was to attack Istanbul (part of modern-day Turkey), the capital of the Ottoman Empire. If they could get the Ottoman Empire to collapse, they could outflank the remaining Central powers. The plan was brilliantly conceived, but poorly executed. It failed, and the war dragged on. And that's when the Allies made the first of three crucial agreements that ultimately changed the course of the Middle East.[4]

A PROMISE TO THE ARABS

In 1962 the cinematic grandeur of Peter O'Toole riding across the Arabian Desert in *Lawrence of Arabia* captivated moviegoers. The film is a highly dramatized yet essentially true story of how British army officer T. E. Lawrence encouraged the Arabs to side with the British and fight against the Ottoman Empire. Lawrence did lead Arab forces on an attack to capture the port of Aqaba. He also tried to convince British officials that Arab independence would benefit England.

To help enlist Arab support, the British High Commissioner in Egypt, Sir Henry McMahon, wrote a letter to Abdullah bin al-Hussein, who would later become the first king of the Hashemite Kingdom of Jordan. In that letter McMahon expressed British approval for an independent Arab state extending across most of the Middle East. "I am empowered in the name of the Government of Great Britain to give the following assurance and make the following reply to your letter: Subject to the above modifications, Great Britain is prepared to recognize and support the independence of the Arabs within the territories in the limits and boundaries proposed by the Sherif of Mecca."[5]

T. E. Lawrence's personal efforts, coupled with this letter from the British High Commissioner, persuaded the Arabs to side with the British against the Ottoman Empire. The die was cast. The promise was made. Arabs accepted at face value the British promise to reward them for their assistance by guaranteeing independence and rightful control over much of the Middle East.

A PROMISE TO THE JEWS

The British faced many problems during World War I. German submarines patrolled the waters around Great Britain, threatening to choke off the sea-lanes, which were the island's lifeline. The Germans also cut off Britain's access to acetone, a solvent used in the production of cordite, the main propellant in bullets and shells. The Germans controlled the production of acetone, so Britain had to find an alternative way to manufacture it. They could very well have lost the war had not the Jewish chemist Chaim Weizmann developed a fermentation process that allowed the British to produce their own acetone.

Weizmann was the right man at the right time for Britain and, so it seemed, for the Jewish people as well. In addition to being a chemist, he was also one of the leaders of Zionism in Britain, a movement committed to establishing a Jewish state or homeland within the boundaries of Palestine. His acetone discovery brought him to the attention of David Lloyd George (Minister of Munitions) and Arthur Balfour (First Lord of the Admiralty) and placed him in a remarkable position of influence. The three developed a friendship that continued after Lloyd George became prime minister and Balfour became foreign secretary.

Weizmann suggested to both men that a permanent Jewish homeland in Palestine had many benefits. It would provide security for the Jewish population already living there, and it would provide a safe haven for Jews trying to escape the war-tattered surroundings of Eastern Europe. A Jewish homeland would benefit the other people of the Middle East by bringing European modernity and scientific advance to an otherwise very backward region of the world. And, he added, the announcement of a Jewish homeland might also help persuade America to join the war effort on the side of the European Allies.

Weizmann proved persuasive.

On November 2, 1917, Arthur Balfour sent a letter to Baron Rothschild, another leader of Britain's Jewish community, detailing Britain's official position on the subject of establishing a permanent Jewish homeland in Palestine. "His Majesty's Government view with favour the establishment in Palestine of a national home for the Jewish people, and will use their best endeavours to facilitate the achievement of this object, it being clearly understood that nothing shall be done which may prejudice the civil and religious rights of existing non-Jewish communities in Palestine, or the rights and political status enjoyed by Jews in any other country."[6]

Jews in Palestine and around the world celebrated and eagerly anticipated the end of the war when Britain would make good on its promise. Unfortunately, the British had now promised parts of the same land to the Arabs and the Jews. To make matters worse, Britain had little intention of honoring *either* promise.

THE SECRET AGREEMENT BETWEEN THE ALLIES

Imagine selling the same home to two different families—making promises to both that are mutually exclusive and that can't possibly be fulfilled. That's exactly what happened to the land of Palestine. It was promised to the Jews and to the Arabs, as both groups already were claiming ancient and even prophetic rights to those territories.

Britain's duplicate promises to the Arabs and Jews are partly responsible for many of the misunderstandings in the Middle East. But it was the third agreement—one the Allies hoped to keep secret—that is most responsible for today's crisis in the Middle East and eventually the rise of the ISIS crisis.

Britain and France decided to quietly carve up the Middle East among themselves!

In May 1916 the British, French, and Russians reached an understanding. Should they succeed in defeating the Ottoman Empire, they planned to divide it among themselves, with most of the territory going to the British and to the French. The agreement was to remain secret. But after the Russian revolution of 1917, the new communist government published all the documents in an effort to embarrass the British and the French.

The Sykes-Picot Agreement, as it was known, carved up much of the Middle East into British and French spheres of influence. The agreement, which was largely adopted during the 1920 San Remo conference following World War I, effectively canceled out or modified much of what had been promised

> Many of the nations in the Middle East are creations of World War I, their borders drawn by Europeans. And they were drawn badly. We're seeing the consequences of that in the conflicts right now.
> **—Richard Engel**
> *NBC Nightly News*[7]

to the Arabs and the Jews. That agreement, more than anything else, fundamentally altered the landscape of the Middle East in two major ways.

COLONIAL INFLUENCE, WESTERN IDEALS

First, the Sykes-Picot Agreement laid the groundwork for aggressive European colonial influence in the Middle East. Each country was allowed to establish direct or indirect control over its designated area of influence. Britain wanted to control an area that would give it a clear path to the oil in the Persian Gulf and to its empire in India. France initially wanted a clear path to the oil fields around Mosul, but they settled instead for control of greater Syria, along with a major share of the Turkish Petroleum Company. These spheres of influence are the reason the second most prominent language spoken (after Arabic) in Lebanon and Syria is French . . . while in Jordan, Saudi Arabia, and Iraq, it is English.

The second way the Sykes-Picot Agreement shaped all subsequent events in the modern Middle East was through trying to impose the Western ideals of nations and nationalism on a region defined by ethnic and religious loyalties. Look closely at the following map of the Middle East, "Middle East Boundaries Set by the Sykes-Picot Agreement." Many of the borders between Syria, Jordan, Iraq, and Saudi Arabia are little more than straight lines drawn on a map. The borders of these countries were determined by European cartographers with little or no consideration for geographical or ethnic boundaries—completely ignorant of the subtle distinctions related to religious or tribal loyalties. In short, the countries created were totally artificial, a recipe for unending conflict and intensifying frustration toward the West.

Middle East Boundaries Set by the Sykes-Picot Agreement

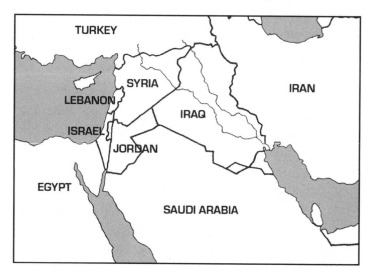

A prime example is Iraq. Most of us have grown up assuming there must have always been a country named Iraq. There wasn't. Prior to World War I the region was actually divided into three separate provinces in the Ottoman Empire, each named after a principal city—Mosul, Baghdad, and Basra. And each region was dominated by a different group: the Kurds in the north, the Sunni Arabs in the center, and the Shiite Arabs in the south.

Britain pushed to have the three provinces cobbled together into the country of Iraq.

Consequently, the area has been a tinderbox of ethnic conflict and racial tension ever since. Iraqi president Saddam Hussein (1979–2003) led a Sunni-dominated government that oppressed the Kurds in the north and the Shiites in the south. More recently the Shiite-dominated government of Nouri al-Malaki oppressed the Kurds and the Sunnis. And it was the Sunni opposition to Mal-aki's government that encouraged so many Sunnis to support ISIS.

In an ironic twist of fate the Great War—the "war to end war" —ultimately plowed, planted, and cultivated the land of the Middle East in a way that has caused it to yield a never-ending crop of con-flict. But to understand how ISIS grew to become one of the most prolific products of that garden, we need to move forward in time to the late 1970s—a time with eerie parallels to what we're experiencing today.

> [Britain and France] created the contemporary Arab world. They played God and produced mutilated entities that almost a century later are coming apart.
> **Fawaz Gerges**
> **London School of Economics and Political Science**

2

THE RISE OF
THE MUJAHIDEEN

History teaches, perhaps, very few clear lessons.
But surely one such lesson learned by the world at great cost
is that aggression, unopposed, becomes a contagious disease.

PRESIDENT JIMMY CARTER
Address to the nation following the Soviet invasion of Afghanistan[1]

America struggles to get back on its feet after pulling its troops home from a long, divisive war. A sputtering economy keeps unemployment above acceptable levels. Prices for food and fuel rise exponentially, putting greater strain on already stretched family budgets. A dysfunctional relationship between the president and Congress threatens the United States' ability to move forward. US hostages are being threatened by Islamic radicals in the Middle East. And a belligerent Russia takes full advantage of the situation to invade one of her neighbors.

In many ways that sounds like today's headlines from Google News. But it is actually a description of 1979. A year that brought stagflation, the partial nuclear meltdown at Three Mile Island near Harrisburg, Pennsylvania, Ayatollah Khomeini and the Iranian Revolution, the Iran hostage crisis, and the Russian invasion of Afghanistan. And because of those last three events, 1979 might also go down as the year that gave birth to modern Islamic fundamentalism.

A YEAR OF TURMOIL

In the Middle East, 1979 careened through highs and lows like a rickety wooden roller coaster. In the spring of that year, Israel and Egypt signed a historic peace treaty, the culmination of the Camp David Accords negotiated between then president Jimmy Carter, Israel's president Menachem Begin, and Egypt's president Anwar Sadat. Egypt emerged as the first Arab state to make peace with Israel, officially recognizing Israel's right to exist as a nation. Less than two years later, members of the Egyptian Islamic Jihad assassinated Sadat in a public display of violence and terror.[2]

While Egypt was playing nice with Israel, the country of Iran was starting to unravel. Eight years after celebrating the 2,500th anniversary of the Persian Empire, the Shah of Iran was forced from his throne and a new Islamic theocracy led by the supreme spiritual leader, Ruhollah Khomeini, was installed. By year's end, *Time* magazine would select Khomeini as "Man of the Year" for 1979. In an ironic twist, this stern and ominous symbol of Islamic intolerance followed the previous year's selection of Anwar Sadat—the man of peace.

A FRAGILE DANCE

In spite of the turmoil in Iran, the overthrow of the Shah might have been little more than a minor historical footnote for most Americans had it not been for what happened next. The deposed shah was allowed into the United States for medical treatment, and Iran demanded his extradition to face charges of murder. America refused, and with Khomeini's blessing, a large group of Iranian students took over the US embassy and held hostage fifty-two American diplomats and citizens for 444 days.

Americans held their breath. Who were these people? How did they compromise our security? And why do they hate us so much? Americans sat bewildered, angry, and in shock. The Iran hostage crisis—and a botched rescue attempt—symbolized the helplessness of the current administration. That debacle by the Carter administration contributed to Ronald Reagan's mammoth defeat of Jimmy Carter in the 1980 presidential election.

While Iran was turning to religious extremism, Iraq moved closer and closer toward a different type of extremism. In 1979 Saddam Hussein formally assumed absolute control over Iraq. The Ba'ath party, a stepchild of the Nazis, was the ruling party in Iraq, rising from the philosophical ashes of National Socialism. The following year Hussein invaded Iran, igniting the eight-year Iran-Iraq war. The delicate dance continued as the United States quietly helped support Iraq as a counterbalance to the rising Iranian threat. Then two years after the Iran-Iraq war ended, Hussein invaded Kuwait.

> Don't listen to those who speak of democracy. They all are against Islam. They want to take the nation away from its mission. We will break all the poison pens of those who speak of nationalism, democracy, and such things.
> **Ayatollah Ruhollah Khomeini[3]**

The year 1979 roared forward. One final event, in December,

took the world by surprise. And one of its unintended consequences was the rise of Islamic jihadists, who ultimately gave birth to ISIS. While the world focused on events unfolding in the Middle East, a thousand miles east of Tehran, soldiers poured south from the Soviet Union into Afghanistan, beginning a nine-year war of occupation.

At the time, the greatest fear in the West was of further Soviet expansion. Just after the 1980 New Year, President Carter addressed the nation to voice his concern. Carter, though visibly shaken and dismayed, described the Soviet invasion as "an extremely serious threat to peace because of the threat of further Soviet expansion into neighboring countries in Southwest Asia and also because such an aggressive military policy is unsettling to other peoples throughout the world."[5] Little did anyone know that in less than a decade the Soviet Union would be forced to retreat from Afghanistan, its military defeated and demoralized. Two years after that the Soviet Union would collapse.

> [Americans] are foolish. They don't understand anything in this world. They never travel. They don't know anything outside the area.
>
> **Saddam Hussein**
> **President of Iraq**[4]

The West *also* failed to realize that the ragtag army of mujahideen, the Islamic guerilla fighters who eventually defeated the Soviet forces, would one day threaten them as well.

THE BIRTH OF TWINS—AND AMERICA'S MOST WANTED

Islamic fundamentalism can trace its modern "birth" to the tumult of 1979. But it was actually the birth of fraternal twins. The first child, *Shiite fundamentalism*, arrived with a great deal of attention from the press. This brand of state-sponsored Islamic fundamentalism emerged in Iran when the shah fled into exile and Khomeini returned in triumph. A national referendum to create a theocratic-republic constitution was held on April 1, 1979—which became the ultimate April Fool's joke on the world. This Shiite/theocratic brand of Islamic fundamentalism was enshrined into law by an overwhelming majority of Iranians. And it has continued on until today.

The second child born that year had a more obscure beginning. Sunni fundamentalism had existed for some time in different countries. One Sunni group, the Egyptian Islamic Jihad, would assassinate Anwar Sadat in 1981. And another group, the Muslim Brotherhood, instigated an uprising against Hafez al-Assad in Hama, Syria, the very next year.

But in many ways the original ancestor of Al-Qaeda and ISIS was born during Russia's occupation of Afghanistan. In response to Russia's invasion, several groups arose from Afghanistan, Pakistan, and a number of Arab countries to drive out the "godless invaders." The fighters soon would be called the mujahideen. Most in the West missed the significance of the name, but it came from the word *jihad*. The mujahideen were *those doing jihad*.

The United States helped arm and fund these holy warriors because at the time the greatest perceived threat was the Soviet Union. The motion picture *Charlie Wilson's War* dramatized the efforts of Texas Democratic Congressman Charlie Wilson and his dogged determination to secure CIA funding to purchase advanced weaponry for the Afghan warriors. When asked why he did it, he responded by describing his visit to a hospital in Afghanistan, treating children maimed by Russian mines. "I left those hospitals determined that as long as I had a breath in my body and was a member of Congress that I was going to do what I could to make the Soviets pay for what they were doing."[6]

America's shadowy funding of the mujahideen, under both the Carter and Reagan administrations, turned Afghanistan into Russia's version of Vietnam—a costly and unpopular war that ultimately helped lead to the demise of the Soviet Union. The philosophy behind American policy at the time was that "the enemy of my enemy is my friend." Russia had helped arm the Viet Cong, so the United States helped arm the mujahideen. But once Russia pulled out of Afghanistan, America's interest in the country faded in the rubble. Without foresight or care, the United States fecklessly left well-armed but splintered groups of Islamic warriors to pick up the pieces, restore order, and attempt to rebuild the country. And one of those mujahideen warriors was a young, wealthy, and radical Saudi national whose name would become a household word and who himself would emerge as America's most wanted criminal.

His name was Osama bin Laden.

CONNECTING THE DOTS

Our task, your task . . . is to try to connect the dots before something happens, not afterwards. People say, "Well, where's the smoking gun?" Well, we don't want to see a smoking gun from a weapon of mass destruction.

DONALD RUMSFELD
United States Secretary of Defense[1]

You can't connect the dots looking forward; you can only connect them looking backwards.

STEVE JOBS
Founder of Apple, Inc.[2]

Most of us have played "dot to dot" or "connect the dots." What begins as a blank page with an apparently random series of dots turns into a face or flower as we draw lines to connect the numbered dots. "Connecting the dots" has even become a metaphor to describe our ability to ferret out significant relationships between apparently random events or objects that enable us to discern an overall pattern.

One of the more involved games of connect the dots might be tracing the pedigrees of thoroughbred horses. A truism in horse racing is that pedigree matters—that a champion racehorse is often as much a product of breeding as it is of training. That's why handicappers pay such close attention to a horse's pedigree. To anticipate how well a horse might run, they look back through its family history and try to connect the genetic dots of past champions.

To understand ISIS we need to follow a similar process and connect the dots in their pedigree.

DOT ONE: THE MUJAHIDEEN

In the 1970s, much like today, Afghanistan was in political turmoil. After four decades in power, the king of Afghanistan was deposed by his cousin, who declared himself the first president of the country. Five years later this new ruler was overthrown and killed in a military coup. The new government set out to make Afghanistan a socialist country. They changed the flag to mirror that of the Soviet Union and began implementing socialist-style reforms.

The reaction of most Afghan people—who were rural, conservative, and Islamic—was very negative. They rebelled against this secular government, which they saw as little more than a puppet whose strings were being pulled by Moscow. Because of growing fears over Russia's continued meddling, the United States began looking for ways to help arm the rebels.

The country of Afghanistan soon was in full revolt against the communist government, which in turn appealed to Moscow for help. That help came in December 1979. For the next eight years the Russians fought an increasingly desperate war against a growing Islamic insurgency. But who were these jihadists who arose to purge Afghanistan of "Soviet infidels"?

In the West we referred to them as mujahideen and as Afghan freedom fighters. Some saw parallels to American colonists rising up against the British during the Revolutionary War. What was less understood at the time was the strong religious motivation of the mujahideen. They weren't fighting for "freedom" in the sense that most in the West understand the word. Instead, they were fighting to expel the godless Soviets from their country and to reestablish conservative Islam and Sharia law.

Most of the mujahideen came from the different tribal groups within Afghanistan. But volunteers from other Muslim countries also came to aid in the fight. One of them was Osama bin Laden, the son of a billionaire Saudi Arabian businessman. Though only in his early twenties, he set up a base to help funnel arms, money, and fighters to Afghanistan, using some of his own funds to help finance the mission.

By 1988 the Soviet forces had been forced out of Afghanistan. The mujahideen had achieved their goal of driving the infidels out! The events that followed lead us to the next dot in this confusing puzzle.

DOT TWO: THE TALIBAN

Afghanistan was free from Soviet domination, but it was a country in crisis. The mujahideen hadn't been a unified army, nor had they been controlled by a central government. The many different groups of jihadists fought for Islam, but ultimately they remained loyal to their own clans or tribes. They had won the war, but the different warlords now began to fight among themselves. This war-weary nation seemed incapable of finding a path to peace. The Taliban rose to power to unite Afghanistan under the banner of Islam.

The origin of the word *Taliban* is as confusing as the group it describes. It's the Pashto or Afghani word for "students." During the Russian invasion of Afghanistan, thousands of Afghani men fled to Pakistan where they received instruction at Islamic schools. They became *students* of a very strict version of Islam. And their founder and spiritual leader was Mohammed Omar.

Mohammed Omar fought with the mujahideen against the Soviet Union and was known as a fearless and ferocious fighter. He was wounded four times in battle, ultimately losing an eye. He traveled to Pakistan, first as a student and later a teacher, in a madrasah, a religious school. After the war Omar moved back to Afghanistan and set up a school there.

The transformation of Mohammed Omar from teacher to Taliban leader is wrapped in mystery. Some say he had a dream in which a woman told him it was his destiny to end the chaos. Another legend is that he led a small group of followers to attack a local warlord because of the brutal sexual exploitation of a child. A less venerable tale says the group arose to control a key route for an oil pipeline. But whatever triggered the transformation from instructor to radical leader, Mohammed Omar brought about a rapid transformation.

> My pledge of allegiance to the Emir of the Believers [Mullah Omar] is the great pledge of allegiance, which is mentioned in the chapters of the Koran and the stories of the Sunnah. Every Muslim should set his mind and heart and pledge allegiance to the Emir of the Believers Mullah Mohammed Omar for this is the great pledge.
>
> **Osama bin Laden**[3]

Beginning in 1994 with a very small but loyal group of followers, Omar quickly defeated several warlords. Others rallied to his side, and by 1996 he had assumed the title of Emir of the Emirate of Afghanistan. Omar set out to transform the country into his personal version of the ideal Islamic state—a state where women were to remain uneducated and covered in burqas, *sharia* law was supreme, and ancient statues of Buddha needed to be destroyed as idols.

One prominent guest moved back to Afghanistan the year Mohammed Omar took control. It was Osama bin Laden, and he pledged his loyalty to Mohammed Omar,

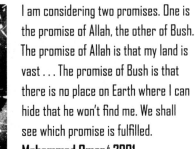

I am considering two promises. One is the promise of Allah, the other of Bush. The promise of Allah is that my land is vast ... The promise of Bush is that there is no place on Earth where I can hide that he won't find me. We shall see which promise is fulfilled.

Mohammed Omar,[4] **2001**

a pledge he publicly acknowledged in 2001. That oath of allegiance, known as *bay'at*, is sanctioned by the Quran as a pledge of loyalty as binding as if it were being made to Allah himself.[5] This loyalty oath to Mohammed Omar was reaffirmed in 2014 by Ayman al-Zawahiri, who replaced bin Laden as head of Al-Qaeda.

The US invasion of Afghanistan in 2001 began that October after the Taliban refused to hand over Osama bin Laden, following the September 11 terrorist attacks on US soil. Mohammed Omar was forced to flee Kabul and go into hiding, and the United States put a $10 million bounty on his head. But America was never able to capture him. We don't even know if he is still alive and where he might be hiding.

The Taliban still pose a threat to the government now ruling Afghanistan. But the Taliban lead us to the next in this series of dots that we must connect in understanding ISIS.

DOT THREE: AL-QAEDA

Sometimes in dot-to-dot puzzles, connecting the different dots produces lines that seem at first to zigzag across the page. Only later do these apparent random lines form the petals of a flower, or the branches of a tree, or a lion's mane. To connect the next dot in our puzzle, we have to move back in time to August 1990 and Saddam Hussein's invasion of Kuwait.

Less than three years after the "godless Soviets" were forced from Afghanistan, an even greater threat to Islam appeared on the horizon. When Saddam Hussein's tanks rolled into Kuwait, much of the West saw it as a brutal invasion by a modern-day despot seeking control over 25 percent of the world's proven oil reserves. Saudi Arabia saw it as a threat to their very existence and invited coalition forces, led by the United States, into their kingdom.

Osama bin Laden saw the military buildup in Saudi Arabia as still another invasion of Muslim lands by oil-hungry Western crusaders. And this invasion was taking place in the country that was home to two of Islam's three holiest cities. He had to purge the Middle East of these Western infidels.

Osama bin Laden is synonymous with Al-Qaeda in the same way Bill Gates is identified with Microsoft or Steve Jobs with Apple. And the comparison is indeed valid because Osama bin Laden was the driving force behind Al-Qaeda. But its roots also go back to Afghanistan and the mujahideen.

Al-Qaeda in Arabic means "the base," and the name originated during bin Laden's time in Afghanistan. The fighters there referred to their training camp as "the base," much as someone in the armed forces today might refer to his or her main post as the "base." Bin Laden officially started Al-Qaeda in 1988, the year the Soviets left Afghanistan, and he moved back to Saudi Arabia soon after. The buildup of Allied forces in Saudi Arabia made the rulers of the country far less tolerant of a religious firebrand preaching against America, so in 1992 bin Laden and his followers moved again to set up operations in Sudan. But after a failed Al-Qaeda attempt to assassinate the president of Egypt, the Egyptians put pressure on Sudan, and bin Laden once again had to move his operations. He chose a place where he knew he would be welcome. Afghanistan.

It was time for Al-Qaeda to launch its campaign to drive the "Crusaders" and the Jews from the Middle East.

Prior to September 11, 2001, few Americans really knew much about Osama bin Laden or Al-Qaeda. The focus had remained intent on Iran and Iraq, and episodic periods of state-sponsored aggression. Apart from airplane hijackings or isolated terrorist incidents, most people in American government did not believe terror organizations were capable of launching major attacks against the United States. But we should have been paying closer attention. Al-Qaeda was becoming more active, more aggressive, and more effective. And their chief target was the United States.

In 1995 Al-Qaeda carried out a car bombing in Saudi Arabia that killed five Americans. Then in 1998 they bombed the US embassies in Kenya and Tanzania, killing more than 200 people and wounding more than 5,000. That same year bin Laden

> The ruling to kill the Americans and their allies—civilians and military—is an individual duty for every Muslim who can do it in any country in which it is possible to do it, in order to liberate the al-Aqsa Mosque and the holy mosque from their grip, and in order for their armies to move out of all the lands of Islam, defeated and unable to threaten any Muslim.
> **Osama bin Laden**
> *Fatwa* issued in 1998

issued a religious *fatwa* (binding religious ruling), calling on Muslims everywhere to kill Americans whenever they can.[6]

Al-Qaeda became more sophisticated, and more deadly. In January 2000 they tried to attack the USS *The Sullivans* but failed. In October 2000 they succeeded in bombing the USS *Cole*, killing seventeen sailors and wounding thirty-nine. And then came September 11, 2001. And suddenly everyone knew about Osama bin Laden and Al-Qaeda. The game had changed.

DOT FOUR: AL-QAEDA IN IRAQ

Virtually everyone has heard of Al-Qaeda, but most don't understand exactly how the group functions. Al-Qaeda began with a centralized leadership under Osama bin Laden. And the attacks in 2000 and 2001 demonstrated that Al-Qaeda was a sophisticated organization capable of planning, organizing, funding, and executing complex terrorist operations. But the invasion of Afghanistan by the United States disrupted Al-Qaeda. Following that, Al-Qaeda's leadership went into hiding, and communication became more difficult.

That's when Al-Qaeda developed into what some have compared to a franchise operation, establishing affiliates in different regions of the world committed to the overall mission but operating semi-independently to fulfill that mission. The new structure resulted in greater operational diversity among the different affiliates. "The franchise model has been essential to the group's survival, even if that means affiliated groups are often left to their own devices and focus more on local struggles than on attacking the West."[7]

One such franchise was the Al-Qaeda branch set up in Iraq following the toppling of Saddam Hussein by the United

States in the spring of 2003. Power and control in Iraq shifted from the Sunnis to the Shiites. America also pursued a policy of "de-Ba'athification"—removing former members of Hussein's Ba'ath party from the government and the military. Unfortunately, this produced two unintended consequences. The Shiite-dominated government came under greater influence from Iran. And the Sunnis who lost power felt marginalized and threatened. They were the ideal "customers" for Al-Qaeda's newest franchise—*Al-Qaeda in Iraq*.

The leader of this franchise was Abu Musab al-Zarqawi, and he set out to make this franchise the most notorious of all. Al-Zarqawi was a wanted man before America invaded Iraq. He spent time in a Jordanian prison, and he later tried to blow up the Radisson hotel in Amman. The possibility that Saddam Hussein was harboring him in Iraq was part of the justification for the US invasion in 2003. Zarqawi was the most dangerous CEO of the most ruthless Al-Qaeda franchise.

What set Al-Qaeda in Iraq apart from other Al-Qaeda affiliates? It was their targets and their methods. Al-Qaeda in Iraq didn't simply target non-Muslims. Instead, they attacked both Americans and Shiite Muslims. Al-Zarqawi, a Sunni, viewed Shiites as Islamic heretics as well as collaborators with America and Iran against the Sunnis.

Al-Zarqawi's methods were equally horrific. His group specialized in suicide bombings, targeting both military and civilians, and killing thousands by using vehicles packed with explosives. Al-Zarqawi also introduced another gruesome practice—beheading as a means of execution. Al-Qaeda in Iraq released a video showing al-Zarqawi beheading an American civilian who had been abducted, and he is thought to have personally beheaded at least one other person.

Beheadings and bombings against non-Sunni Muslims became the hallmark of Al-Qaeda in Iraq. But under al-Zarqawi the organization maintained its loyalty to Al-Qaeda.

After a brutal three-year campaign of terror, al-Zarqawi was killed in June 2006 in a targeted air attack. The head of Al-Qaeda in Iraq had been eliminated. And with the death of Osama bin Laden, it looked as if the United States had finally won the war against Al-Qaeda and its affiliates. President Obama declared war over in Iraq and nearly over in Afghanistan: "Thanks to [the] sacrifice and service of our brave men and women in uniform, the war in Iraq is over, the war in Afghanistan is winding down, Al-Qaeda has been decimated, and Osama bin Laden is dead."

Unfortunately, Al-Qaeda in Iraq was still alive, and al-Zarqawi's eventual replacement proved to be even more vicious than his predecessor.

DOT FIVE: ISIS

After al-Zarqawi's death, the *Al-Qaeda in Iraq* franchise went into a period of decline. The US troop surge in Iraq along with the rise of the "Sons of Iraq"—Sunni tribal sheikhs who worked with the US military to stabilize the region— brought a measure of calm to Anbar Province. Unfortunately, once America's forces withdrew, the Shiite-dominated government in Baghdad disbanded these "Awakening" groups and dissatisfaction among the Sunnis was again on the rise.

In 2010 the Al-Qaeda in Iraq franchise had another "opening at the top." Combined US and Iraqi forces killed the top two Al-Qaeda operatives in Iraq. At the time, Vice President Joseph Biden called their deaths "potentially devastating blows to Al-Qaida [in] Iraq."[8] But the celebration was premature.

Two events caused the cancer that was Al-Qaeda in Iraq to reappear and eventually metastasize.

The first was the appointment in May 2010 of Abu Bakr al-Baghdadi as head of the Islamic State of Iraq, as Al-Qaeda in Iraq was now known. Al-Baghdadi had originally helped found a militant group that became part of the Mujahideen Shura Council, an umbrella group of six Sunni Islamist groups fighting in Iraq. His background made him a natural successor to al-Zarqawi, or so it must have seemed to members of Al-Qaeda.

The second event was the *Arab Spring* uprisings against entrenched governments, which originated in Tunisia seven months later and began sweeping across the Arab world. By February 2011 President Hosni Mubarak was forced from office in Egypt, and by August, Muammar Gaddafi was overthrown in Libya. Protests started in Syria in March 2011, but they failed to bring about the collapse of the Syrian government. Instead, a bloody, protracted civil war began that killed more than two hundred thousand Syrians and forced half the population to flee their homes as refugees. The conflict ultimately became a struggle between the rebel groups representing the Sunni majority and the government of Bashar al-Assad, a Shiite-affiliated dictator propped up by Iran and Russia. That combustible mixture of religious and ethnic tension only needed a spark to set it all ablaze. And al-Baghdadi supplied that spark.

Al-Baghdadi moved his forces from Iraq into northern Syria to join the fight against the Syrian government. He brought along his group's fanatical hatred for all who didn't follow its brand of Islam. And he also brought along the group's brutal tactics—suicide bombings and beheadings. While the rest of the world focused on the other Islamic groups fighting in western Syria, al-Baghdadi's group carved out a kingdom along Syria's border with Iraq.

The death of Osama bin Laden in 2011 created a crisis of leadership for Al-Qaeda. Many of the Al-Qaeda affiliates, including Al-Qaeda in Iraq, now known as the Islamic State of Iraq, had pledged their loyalty to him. Ayman al-Zawahiri, bin Laden's successor, was less dynamic and less charismatic. And it showed. Like Frankenstein, he wasn't able to control the monster he had helped create. The split finally came in Syria.

The official Al-Qaeda affiliate in Syria was the al-Nusra Front. Created in 2012, it had been the most successful of the groups fighting against the Syrian army. But in 2013 al-Baghdadi released a tape announcing that al-Nusra was combining with his group, which was now to be known as ISIS or ISIL.[9] Unfortunately, al-Baghdadi hadn't bothered to inform al-Nusra—or Al-Qaeda Central—about this announcement before it became public! Al-Nusra rejected the "merger," and Al-Qaeda Central sent a letter to both groups saying the two franchises were separate . . . and were *not* to be combined. The letter read, in part, "Sheikh Abu Bakr al-Baghdadi was wrong when he announced the Islamic State in Iraq and the Levant without asking permission or receiving advice from us and even without notifying us."[10]

This very public rebuke from al-Zawahiri was a crisis for ISIS. Al-Baghdadi responded by rejecting the ruling and announcing the merger *was* going to move forward, in effect launching a "hostile takeover" of one Al-Qaeda franchise by another. Al-Qaeda Central responded by announcing it was disbanding the Al-Qaeda franchise in Iraq. ISIS rejected the ruling, and the Islamic equivalent of a corporate power struggle ensued. The two groups finally split and ISIS declared the formation of the Islamic State, a Muslim caliphate, with al-Baghdadi as the new caliph, or leader.

Al-Qaeda had been focused on liberating Muslim lands from the Western "Crusaders" and Jews, but ISIS had even greater ambitions. Their goal wasn't just to overthrow the governments of Iraq and Syria but to replace them with the ideal Islamic state. Fed from the radical and violent teachings within the Quran, ISIS pursued its violent advance to conquer a territory stretching from the Euphrates River to deep expanses of North Africa. It wanted to establish a state devoid of all infidels—Jews, Christians, Shiites, Yazidis, Druze, and Alawites—anyone unwilling to submit to their austere brand of radical Islam.

The rest is history.

AN INCOMPLETE PICTURE

The picture is almost complete. The dots lead from Afghanistan to Iraq. From the mujahideen to ISIS. From expelling infidels to establishing a caliphate. But does the picture remain incomplete, or are there additional dots yet to be connected?

The West has shown a remarkable ability to focus so intently on one crisis that it ignores a greater threat bubbling beneath the surface. Could the current ISIS crisis morph yet again into something even more dangerous?

There is certainly a very real danger that we could become too focused on ISIS. If we become mesmerized by them, we might miss other threats. More recently a so-called lone-wolf terrorist attacked the Jewish Museum in Brussels, Belgium, killing four people. The attacker, Mehdi Nemmouche, was a French citizen who had fought in Syria for ISIS.[11] Hundreds, perhaps thousands, of individuals with Western passports are now part of the ISIS army and could someday return home to carry out their own personal jihad.

As of this writing, a group of former Al-Qaeda members named Khorasan is recruiting jihadists from the West to carry out suicide bombings using sophisticated explosives proving much more difficult to detect. And like the bombs they're developing, this group—until very recently—remained largely undetected.

ISIS itself has called on Muslims around the world to take violent action against "unbelievers." In a hint of what could follow, Australia announced it had uncovered an ISIS-inspired plot to behead civilians randomly on the streets and capture the brutal acts on video. Two separate terrorist attacks in Canada, just days apart, killed two Canadian soldiers. And these are but the tip of the iceberg of a radical Islamic war being waged against the West.

The ISIS crisis is real. ISIS thrives on its ability to create immense levels of fear and confusion. Unfortunately, such responses can lead to prejudice, paranoia, or even paralysis. Like Britain at the start of Second World War, this is a time when we need to "keep calm and carry on."

If you can kill a disbelieving American or European—especially the spiteful and filthy French—or an Australian, or a Canadian or any other disbeliever from the disbelievers waging war . . . kill him in any manner or way however it may be.
Audio recording from the Islamic State, September 2014

Understanding the reality of the Middle East in greater detail can help us respond rationally and wisely and perhaps avoid the mistakes of our past.

4

THE RULE OF HATE

Jews are the historic enemies of Muslims
and carry the greatest hatred for the nation of Muhammad.

MUSLIM BROTHERHOOD STATEMENT[1]

Although much diversity exists among Islamic sects in the Middle East, the variant Muslim factions seem to share one common belief: a visceral hatred of all Jewish people and of Israel. Even where there are seeming exceptions, the exceptions seem to prove the rule.

For example, Egypt made peace with Israel, and Egyptian president Anwar Sadat was assassinated for taking that bold step. King Abdullah I of Jordan was at least open to a Jewish presence in the Promised Land; and his grandson, King Hussein, eventually did make peace. But Abdullah was also killed, and King Hussein had to survive a series of attempted assassinations and coups. No leader in the Middle East is safe who stands in any way with Israel.

WHEN HATRED RULES

Sunni or Shiite, pro-Western or anti-Western, a common thread across the Muslim world is a loathing of Jews and Israel. During World War II, US president Franklin Roosevelt contacted King Ibn Sa'ud of Saudi Arabia about a possible negotiated settlement between the Arabs and Jews in Palestine. King Sa'ud responded that he was "prepared to receive anyone of any religion except (repeat except) a Jew."[2] Over sixty years later Ayatollah Khamenei, the supreme leader of the Shiite branch of Islam, spewed his own personal hatred for Israel in rather graphic terms when he declared that, "Iran's position, which was first expressed by the Imam [Khomeini] and stated several times by those responsible, is that the cancerous tumor called Israel must be uprooted from the region."[3]

But why the hatred? The answer may surprise you.

JEWISH SETTLEMENTS ARE NOT THE CAUSE

A perception is often held that hatred between Muslims and Jews stems from the establishment of Jewish settlements, either settlements established before 1948 or those built after the capture of the West Bank during the 1967 Six-Day War. They would argue that by building on this land, and dispossessing the Arabs who lived there, Israel sowed the seeds of conflict that have been sprouting ever since.

Yet Muslim hatred of the Jewish people in the Middle East existed *before* the Six-Day War. It existed *before* the birth of Israel in 1948. It existed *before* the United Nations voted to partition Palestine into two countries in 1947. In fact, "even before the Mandate for Palestine was assigned to Great Britain by the Allies at the San Remo Conference (April 1920) and endorsed by the League of Nations (July 1922), Palestinian Arabs were carrying out organized attacks against Jewish communities in Palestine."[4]

As Jewish people were returning to the land of Palestine in the late 1800s and early 1900s, Arab Muslims were streaming into the land as well. In 1920 the population for the whole of Palestine was just over 700,000. Eighty percent were Muslim, 10 percent were Arab Christian, and 10 percent were Jewish. By 1948 the population had swelled to 1.9 million. Over 600,000 were Jewish, reflecting a significant influx of Jewish refugees who fled to Palestine to escape persecution in Europe.

But Jews weren't the only ones whose population in Palestine was increasing because of immigration. The large increase in the Arab population was also due, in part, to an influx of immigrants. "After remaining nearly stagnant for centuries, the population exploded in modern times due to improved infrastructure, agriculture, and immigration, both Jewish and Arab . . . The Arab population of Palestine grew more from 1922 to 1947 than it had over the previous 400 years."[5]

The Royal Institute for International Affairs, when reporting on the growth of the Arab population during the 1920s and 1930s, noted that "the number of Arabs who have entered Palestine illegally from Syria and Transjordan is unknown. But probably considerable."[6]

ANGER IN THE NAME OF ALLAH

The Muslim opposition to a Jewish presence in the land was never just about settlements—whether in the West Bank or in the previously under-occupied land along the coast. That hatred began long before "settlements" appeared and ultimately was a conflict over the question of whether any kind of Jewish entity could arise and control land that had been conquered

Arise, o sons of Arabia. Fight for your sacred rights. Slaughter Jews wherever you find them. Their spilled blood pleases Allah, our history and religion. That will save our honor.

Haj Amin al-Husseini
Grand Mufti of Jerusalem[8]

on behalf of Allah. Again Morris reveals that "the Jewish state had arisen at the heart of the Muslim Arab world—and that world could not abide it."[7]

The issue wasn't about settlements but about whose God was sovereign.

BACK TO MUHAMMAD

After Muhammad fled from Mecca to Medina, he had contact with the large Jewish population in that area. He initially viewed the Jews and Christians as "people of the Book," and he expected them to understand and accept his new "revelation" from God. But both groups rejected his message. The Jews refused to accept Muhammad as a prophet, and they didn't accept the Quran's misappropriation of Jewish people and events for Islam. This wholesale rejection of Muhammad's claims changed everything.

Once it was clear Jews would not accept him, Muhammad began to minimize or eliminate the Jewish influence on his beliefs. For example, he shifted the direction of prayers from Jerusalem to Mecca, made Friday his special day of prayer, and renounced the Jewish dietary laws (except for the prohibition on eating pork). Originally, he said the Arabs were descendants of Abraham through his son Ishmael, but in the Quran Abraham's connection to the Jews is denied, with Muhammad asserting Abraham to be only the patriarch of Islam, not Judaism, because Abraham "surrendered himself to Allah."[9]

Muhammad turned against the Jewish clans living in Medina. Some he forcibly expelled. The others were attacked.

Muhammad eventually killed the Jewish men who refused to convert, enslaved their wives and children, and confiscated their property. The pattern of brutality and violence the world is presently witnessing with ISIS can trace its roots all the way back to the beginnings of Islam— all the way back to Muhammad.

When our enemies usurp some Islamic lands, Jihad becomes a duty binding on all Muslims. In order to face the usurpation of Palestine by the Jews, we have no escape from raising the banner of Jihad.
Hamas Charter
Article Fifteen

REVELATIONS FROM BEYOND

In fact, in his later "revelations" Muhammad shared what he believed to be God's complete displeasure with the Jews, a principle he used to justify his hatred for all who refuse to name Allah as the one true God. Here are some of the statements against the Jews found in the Quran.

- "And we did certainly give Moses the Torah and followed up after him with messengers. And we gave Jesus, the son of Mary, clear proofs and supported him with the Pure Spirit. But is it [not] that every time a messenger came to you, [O Children of Israel], with what your souls did not desire, you were arrogant? And a party [of messengers] you denied and another party you killed. And they said, 'Our hearts are wrapped.' *But, [in fact], Allah has cursed them for their disbelief,* so little is it that they believe" (2:87–88, emphasis added).
- "Whoever is an enemy to *Allah and His angels and His messengers and Gabriel and Michael—then indeed, Allah is an enemy to the disbelievers*" (2:98, emphasis added).

- "O, you who have believed, do not take the Jews and the Christians as allies. They are [in fact] allies of one another. And whoever is an ally to them among you—then indeed, he is [one] of them. Indeed, Allah guides not the wrongdoing people" (5:51).
- "Say, 'Shall I inform you of [what is] worse than that as penalty from Allah? [It is that of] *those whom Allah has cursed and with whom He became angry and made of them apes and pigs and slaves of Taghut [Satan].* Those are worse in position and further astray from the sound way'" (5:60, emphasis added).
- "And the Jews say, 'The hand of Allah is chained.' *Chained are their hands, and cursed are they for what they say.* Rather, both His hands are extended; He spends however He wills. And that which has been revealed to you from your Lord [Allah] will surely increase many of them in transgression and disbelief. *And we have cast among them animosity and hatred until the Day of Resurrection.* Every time they kindled the fire of war [against you], Allah extinguished it. And they strive throughout the land [causing] corruption, and Allah does not like corrupters" (5:64, emphasis added).

In addition to the Quran, Muslims accept the *Hadith*, the collected oral traditions of the words and deeds of Muhammad reported by his early followers. The material is extensive, and the two branches of Islam accept different sets of collections. But the Hadith expresses, in lurid detail, Muhammad's description of God's undiminished hatred for the Jewish people. For example, "The last hour would not come unless the Muslims will fight against the Jews and the Muslims would kill them until the Jews would hide themselves behind a stone or a tree and a stone or a tree would say: 'Muslim, or the servant of Allah, there is a Jew behind me; come and kill him'" (Sahih Muslim 41:6985).

ONLY ONE REAL NATION

At its core, Islam holds to a form of replacement theology. This is a belief that Jews and Christians were indeed once God's chosen people, but He rejected them for refusing to accept God's prophets. The Christians didn't accept Muhammad, but Jewish people rejected *both* Jesus and Muhammad. Because of that rejection Christians and Jews are under God's judgment. And they are both to be vehemently opposed.

According to one Hadith, Muhammad, while on his deathbed, cursed the Jews and Christians for building places of worship at the prophets' graves: "When the last moment of the life of Allah's Apostle came he started putting his 'Khamisa' on his face and when he felt hot and short of breath he took it off his face and said, 'May Allah curse the Jews and Christians for they built the places of worship at the graves of their Prophets'" (Sahih Bukhari 1:8:427).

Another Hadith claims Muslims will be spared from hell by having God appoint Jews and Christians to take their place in the hellfire: "Abu Musa reported that Allah's Messenger (May peace be upon him) said: 'When it will be the Day of Resurrection Allah would deliver to every Muslim a Jew or a Christian and say: "That is your rescue from Hell-Fire"'" (Sahih Muslim 37:6665).

Islam ultimately views Christians and Jews as enemies of Allah, but it is the Jews who now occupy land Muslims believe rightfully belongs to Allah and his followers. And that makes the Jews the one enemy against which all Muslims can unite.

You need to know that ISIS radicals share this hatred for the Jews and for anyone who will simply not convert to its ways. Yet their extreme brand of hatred remains unprecedented among these radical groups. In the words of US Secretary of State John Kerry following the gruesome murder of American aid worker Peter Kassig: "This conflict is not between one civilization and another. . . . This conflict is between civilization itself and barbarism."[10]

And it's a barbarism in a most horrifyingly extreme form, but one that has as its origin a hatred radical Muslims have possessed for generations.

5

A KINGDOM DIVIDED AGAINST ITSELF: SUNNIS VS. SHIITES

If you know yourself but not the enemy,
for every victory gained you will also suffer a defeat.

SUN TZU
Chinese General, sixth century BC[1]

Americans typically do poorly in geography and history. We are a forward-looking nation, more focused on the newest fashion trend or latest electronic device than on understanding details of the past. Part of the reason is a narcissistic, self-focused sense of national importance. But part of the reason is also a lack of education. For example, one-third of all high school administrators reported that their school didn't offer a single course in geography.[2]

But someone might respond, "So what? Does it really matter how much the average American knows about geography or history?" A *Washington Post* survey taken after Russia's invasion of Ukraine suggests it matters a great deal.

In a national sample of 2,066 Americans, the *Post* survey asked what action the United States should take in Ukraine, at the same time asking those sampled to locate Ukraine on a map. Only one out of six Americans could actually find Ukraine on that map. Worse yet, the "farther their guesses were from Ukraine's actual location, the more they wanted the U.S. to intervene with military force."[3]

An uninformed public can pressure its leaders into making poor strategic choices! What we all need is understanding in order to respond to ISIS rationally and with resolve.

BACK TO THE BEGINNING

To understand the ISIS crisis, we must first understand the rise of Islam. And that begins with Muhammad, its prophet.

Muhammad was a forty-year-old wealthy businessman living in Mecca in what is today Saudi Arabia when he began having visions in AD 610. These visions, which continued through his life, ultimately became the seedbed of the Quran. Early on, Muhammad preached to the people of Mecca a message of peace. He had little resources and not a very strong following, and his visions were for the most part peaceful and mundane. Something changed as fewer and fewer responded.

In AD 622 Muhammad traveled 250 miles north from Mecca to Medina. Today the beginning of that trek, known as the *Hijra*, marks the beginning of the Islamic calendar. In that period Muhammad's visions had grown more intense and violent—and his message and ways followed. Eight years later Muhammad marched back to Mecca with an army of ten thousand followers and captured the city. By the time of his death in AD 632, Muhammad's followers had established Islam as a formidable influence throughout much of the Arabian Peninsula.

THE MAKING OF TWO VERSIONS OF ISLAM

Muhammad's death, though, brought the first major crisis for Islam. Who would succeed the prophet as leader? One group, which would become the *Sunnis*, felt it should be the close friend of Muhammad, his father-in-law, Abu Bakr. Another group, the *Shiites*, felt Muhammad himself had determined his successor to be from his own family, and that he had personally chosen his cousin and son-in-law, Ali ibn Abi Talib. Ali was one of Muhammad's closest lifelong supporters and allies. He was also a blood relative.

Had Muhammad intended for this new political and religious empire to be ruled by the most capable successor (his father-in-law), or was Islam intended to be ruled by a member of the family dynasty (his cousin)? Those two opposing approaches to succession split Islam right down the middle.

THE SUNNIS: FOLLOWERS OF ABU BAKR

Many of Muhammad's followers in Medina felt Abu Bakr ought to be the next leader because of his unique ability to articulate the values of Islam and on account of his personal piety. He was therefore elected the first *caliph*, from the Arabic word for "successor." He represented to all around him the *experience* of Muhammad and thus embodied the essence of Islam. Those who accepted Abu Bakr as their new leader eventually became known as Sunnis.

Sunni comes from the word for "custom or tradition" and refers to those who followed the tradition of the prophet and accepted the decision of the majority. Sunni Muslims are the "traditionalists" in the sense that they believe they are the true followers of the customs and traditions as originally instituted by Muhammad and his companions. Members of Al-Qaeda and ISIS come from the Sunni branch of Islam.

THE SHIITES: FOLLOWERS OF ALI

Shiite Muslims trace their roots back to those who believe Muhammad intended his son-in-law and cousin, Ali ibn Abi Talib, to be his rightful successor. For Shiites the successor must be from the direct lineage of Muhammad. The name *Shiite* comes from the Arabic phrase *shi'atu Ali*, which means "the partisans of Ali." They are the Muslims who accepted Ali, not Abu Bakr, as the legitimate heir to Muhammad. They also believed all future leaders were to come from the line of Ali and his wife Fatima, who was Muhammad's daughter.

THE SPLIT WIDENS

If the difference between the Sunnis and Shiites focused only on matters of succession, then it would seem that the split eventually healed. Ali might not have been chosen as the first caliph following the death of Muhammad, but he *was* eventually chosen. Twenty-four years after Muhammad's death, Ali became the successor as the fourth caliph of Islam, theoretically assuming authority over both groups.

Yet, though united under a single head, two events kept the festering sore from healing over. The first was a civil war within Islam itself. The new religion had expanded from the Arabian Peninsula and now included Syria, Persia, and Egypt. That rapid growth brought with it racial and ethnic tensions as the different factions battled for control. The third caliph was murdered, and Ali was selected as the next ruler. Though deeply pious, his rigid, puritanical style of leadership hindered his ability to smooth over the growing rifts. Ali was eventually murdered, and his son Hasan chosen to replace him as caliph. But the cracks that had been forming within Islam expanded into a major crevice.

Another Islamic dynasty based in Damascus forced Hasan from power. What emerged was a new ruling force: the Umayyad caliphate. The ruler of this new dynasty eventually arranged to have Hasan murdered, thus eliminating him as a future potential threat.

The second event that split Sunnis and Shiites is closely related to the first. Ali had stipulated that the next caliph was to be one of his sons, connecting the line of succession directly back to Muhammad. But the caliph who replaced Ali's son Hasan had no such direct connection, making him illegitimate in the eyes of Ali's partisans. And when this new caliph died and was succeeded by his own son, Ali's youngest son joined with others in refusing to accept his authority. That rift led to a second civil war.

At the battle of Karbala (in modern-day Iraq) in AD 680, the new caliph killed and then beheaded Ali's youngest son, Hussein. He also killed Hussein's six-month-old son. The action deeply offended the followers of Ali. It represented another ominous foreshadowing of the horrifying violence to come, the likes of which we are witnessing today by ISIS.

The split within Islam was now complete.

OTHER DIFFERENCES

Over time, other differences developed between the two branches of Islam. Sunnis are led by *imams*, spiritual overseers considered spiritually wise, but not infallible. The Shiites believe their religious leaders (mujtahids and ayatollahs) *are* infallible, as they are direct descendants of Ali and Muhammad. In some ways their view is similar to the Roman Catholic understanding of the pope speaking *ex cathedra*. That's why, in Shiite-ruled Iran, Ayatollah Khamenei is the supreme leader, exerting virtual control over all branches of government and Iranian life.

Sunnis and Shiites both believe in an Islamic redeemer called the *Mahdi*—a Messiah-like figure, who will be joined by Jesus, to rule on earth before the day of judgment. But there is one major difference. Sunnis are waiting for the Mahdi to appear in the future, while the Shiites teach he is already here but hidden. Shiites also believe there have been twelve successors to the prophet Muhammad. Ali was the first in this line, and the twelfth and final imam is Muhammad ibn al-Hasan, also known as Muhammad al-Mahdi.

The Two Branches of Islam

	Sunni	Shiite
Muhammad's successor (relationship)	Abu Bakr (father-in-law)	Ali ibn Abi Talib (cousin and son-in-law)
Leadership criterion	most qualified (chosen by consensus)	descendant by blood
Proponents	Al-Qaeda, ISIS	Ayatollah Khomeini
Present leaders	*imams*	*mujtahids* and *ayatollahs*
Authority among their followers	wise but fallible	infallible
Followers in Middle East	75 to 80%	20 to 25%

This twelfth imam was born in AD 869 and became the final imam when he was just five years old. For several decades he remained hidden and only communicated with his followers through his deputies. After ruling for seventy-two years, he supposedly sent his followers a letter saying he was going into "occultation," or hiding, and wouldn't reappear until sometime in the future, whenever Allah decided. Shiites believe the Mahdi has remained alive, but hidden, all these years.

Sunnis and Shiites do agree that Islam extends from Muhammad to the Mahdi. But how Muhammad's successor was to be selected, and when the Mahdi will appear, are major points of disagreement. And in more recent times, a third area of disagreement has surfaced. In Sunni-dominated countries, the religious leaders, or imams, are under state control. But in Iran the state is under the control of the religious leader.

SUNNIS AND SHIITES ON THE MAP—AND WHY IT MATTERS

There are 1.5 billion Muslims worldwide. Of that number 85 to 90 percent are Sunnis and 10 to 15 percent are Shiites. However, that's not quite the whole story, especially when focusing on the Middle East. Nearly 660 million (over 44 percent) of all Sunni Muslims live in four countries *outside* the Middle East—Bangladesh, India, Indonesia, and Pakistan. If one focuses directly on the Middle East, the number of Shiite Muslims there rises to 20 to 25 percent.

The ratio of Sunnis to Shiites doesn't remain constant among the different countries in the Middle East. Instead, the Shiites are concentrated in several specific geographical regions. These different concentrations crossing international boundaries help explain some of the religious and ethnic tension in countries like Iraq, Syria, and Lebanon.

Distribution of Sunni and Shiite Muslims in the Middle East

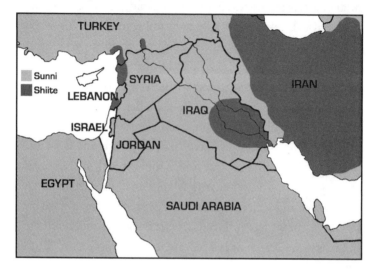

Sunnis and Shiites represent two very different sides of Islam. Both are committed to spreading Islam throughout the world. Both are looking for the appearing of the Mahdi who will precede the day of judgment. Both have produced terrorist groups committed to waging jihad against Israel and the West. And both are deeply suspicious of the other, viewing each other as religious deviants.

In its report "The Sunni-Shia Divide," the Council on Foreign Relations, a think tank specializing in US foreign policy and international affairs, concluded: "An ancient religious divide is helping fuel a resurgence of conflicts in the Middle East and Muslim countries. Struggles between Sunni and Shia forces have fed a Syrian civil war that threatens to transform the map of the Middle East, spurred violence that is fracturing Iraq, and widened fissures in a number of tense Gulf countries."[4]

The "ISIS Crisis" is fundamentally a religious battle. And to avoid making mistakes in facing this threat, the West, including the United States, needs to understand the differences between these two groups. Otherwise, as Chinese general Sun Tzu said, "If you know yourself but not the enemy, for every victory gained you will also suffer a defeat."[5]

6

VARIATIONS ON A THEME: THE COMPOSITION OF ISLAM

Egyptians have inspired us, and they've done so by putting the lie to the idea that justice is best gained through violence. For in Egypt, it was the moral force of nonviolence—not terrorism, not mindless killing—but nonviolence, moral force that bent the arc of history toward justice once more.[1]

PRESIDENT BARAK OBAMA
February 2011

The Arab Spring has become the Arab Winter.[2]

PRESIDENTIAL CANDIDATE MITT ROMNEY

When President Obama addressed the nation from the White House in September 2014 to launch his war against the Islamic State, he started by emphasizing two major points. "ISIL is not 'Islamic.'. . . And ISIL is certainly not a state."[3] By separating ISIS from Islam, the president was trying to deflect the charge that this was to be a war against Muslims. And by not identifying ISIS as a state, he was brushing aside the need for UN Security Council approval prior to launching attacks. There was a clear purpose for the president emphasizing both points.

But were his statements completely accurate?

IS ISIS ISLAMIC?

President Obama stated that ISIS wasn't Islamic because "No religion condones the killing of innocents. And the vast majority of ISIL's victims have been Muslim."[4] Unfortunately, neither argument is fully supported by the Quran nor by Islamic history. It ultimately depends on how a person defines "innocent" and "Muslim."

The Quran contains a story about Moses following a man to learn wisdom from his actions. At one point the man kills a young boy. Moses questions why he had "killed a pure soul." Later the man "enlightens" Moses by sharing his reason for killing the boy. "And as for the boy, his parents were believers, and we feared that he would overburden them by transgression and disbelief. So we intended that their Lord should substitute for them one better than him in purity and nearer to mercy" (18:74, 80–81).

This passage provides the underpinning for honor killings in Islam because it seems to justify the killing of a child if he or she brings shame to the parents.

One incident from early in Muhammad's leadership suggests he viewed someone's innocence or guilt based on their apparent support or opposition to his teaching. After the Battle of the Trench in AD 627, Muhammad attacked the Jewish clan of Qurayza, whom he felt had broken its alliance with him. After a monthlong siege the group surrendered. While the exact number is uncertain, Muhammad evidently beheaded every male (above the age of puberty) in the clan and enslaved all the women and remaining children. *The History of Al-Tabari* records the event.

> They [the Jews] were made to come down, and the Messenger of God [Muhammad] imprisoned them. . . . The Messenger of God went out into the marketplace of Medina (it is still its marketplace today) and had trenches dug in it; then he sent for them and had them beheaded in those trenches. They were brought out to him in groups. . . . They numbered 600 or 700—the largest estimate says they were between 800 and 900. As they were being taken in groups to the Messenger of God, they said . . . , "What do you think will be done to us?" [He] said, "On each occasion you do not understand. Do you not see that the summoner does not discharge [anyone] and that those of you who are taken away do not come back? By God, it is death!" The affair continued until the Messenger of God had finished with them.[5]

This Jewish tribe didn't actually attack Muhammad, but neither had the tribe come to his aid. And it's likely that some in the clan had even argued for supporting him. But in the end every adult male was killed. And this mass beheading by Muhammad eerily foreshadows the beheadings by ISIS today.

President Obama stressed that many of those being killed by ISIS are Muslims, and the Quran does prohibit a Muslim from taking the life of another Muslim in certain situations. "But whoever kills a believer [fellow Muslim] intentionally—his recompense is Hell, wherein he will abide eternally, and Allah has become angry with him and has cursed him and has prepared for him a great punishment" (4:93).

So does the killing of fellow Muslims make ISIS non-Islamic? Not necessarily.

Islam has a history of persecuting and killing "heretics" and "apostates"—those alleged to have departed from the true path of faith in either word or deed. (Sadly, Christianity has a similarly dark history.) And such "heresy" is *still* punishable by death in a number of Muslim countries. In 1989 the government of Iran issued a *fatwa* (official religious edict) ordering the death of author Salman Rushdie because of his book *The Satanic Verses*. In 2014 a Sudanese court convicted Mariam Ibrahim of apostasy and sentenced her to death for refusing to renounce her Christian faith. (Because her father was a Muslim, she was legally considered to be a Muslim as well.) Intense international pressure finally secured her release, but many in Sudan still believed she should have been put to death.

But are all Muslims murdered by ISIS guilty of apostasy? Have they denounced Islam? ISIS would say yes. Many of those they are killing are Shiites and Alawites (an offshoot of the Shiites). To ISIS they are apostates who deserve to die. Make no mistake, much of the fighting in Syria and Iraq is sectarian. The BBC Middle East bureau recently noted that "the current conflicts in Iraq and Syria have also acquired strong sectarian overtones. Young Sunni men in both countries have joined rebel groups, many of which echo the hardline ideology of al-Qaeda."[6]

DEATH TO THE WESTERNER

ISIS also believes the Quran permits them to kill Muslims who support the West. "O you who have believed, do not take the Jews and the Christians as allies. They are [in fact] allies of one another. And whoever is an ally to them among you—then indeed, he is [one] of them. Indeed, Allah guides not the wrongdoing people" (5:51).

Their logic goes something like this: The current governments in Syria and Iraq were established and propped up by the Christian West. The Christians and Jews have caused most of the problems Muslims face in the Middle East today. And thus since Allah does condemn any Muslims who side with the Christians and Jews, it is permissible to kill such Muslims.

ISIS's murder of fellow Muslims and Christians is brutal, harsh, and extreme. But, at least by their understanding, it is not un-Islamic.

IS ISIS A STATE?

As mentioned earlier, ISIS stands for the *Islamic State of Iraq and Syria*. In his statement at the White House, President Obama claimed that ISIS wasn't a state. He pointed to two realities as proof. The first focused on the group's checkered origin and the second its lack of external recognition. Since ISIS "was formerly al-Qaeda's affiliate in Iraq . . . it is recognized by no government, nor by the people it subjugates." But are these valid criteria for determining whether or not ISIS is a state?

Evil movements have grown into recognized states. The National Socialist party in Germany was just a small gang of thugs who took advantage of troubled times to eventually establish the Third Reich. And Vladimir Lenin led the Communist

Party in its takeover of Russia. It's not where a group starts but where it ends up that determines whether it is successful in building a state.

Certainly one criterion for being a nation is having others recognize your existence. But does the lack of international recognition mean ISIS is not a nation? In 1948 no Arab country recognized the existence of Israel, but the nation was established. And though the People's Republic of China came into existence in 1949, the United States didn't formally recognize it until 1979. International recognition is helpful, but not essential, in establishing a state.

President Obama's second point seemed to have more validity. He said ISIS wasn't a state because those under its rule are conquered subjects, not willing citizens. But ISIS does seem to have some measure of support from Sunnis living in the area they now control. And it's a sad reality of history that many nations have conquered and subjugated minority groups. It's not right or fair, but it's also not as strong an argument against ISIS being a state as some, like President Obama, wish to believe.

So when does a movement develop into a state? Is it when it receives membership in the United Nations, or when it can issue recognized passports? By those criteria ISIS will likely never be a state. But could a state be defined by its ability to enact and enforce laws, impose taxes, provide social services, field an army, or define and defend controlled borders? By those measures, ISIS is closer to being a state than some countries already holding a seat at the UN General Assembly.

So what are the basic criteria for establishing a legitimate government? Could the Middle East be using a different yardstick?

RECOGNIZED GOVERNMENTS IN
THE MIDDLE EAST: THREE KINDS

For over a century 3-In-One Oil has been a go-to part of life—America's "tool kit in a can," according to the company slogan. The iconic red-and-white squeezable can has found a home on countless shelves and workbenches. But "3-In-One" might also be a good way to describe the governments of most Islamic countries. There seem to be three varying styles of government in the Middle East. But the dominant melody line that winds its way through each variation is Islam.

I. DEMOCRATIC ISLAM

The first in the variety of Islamic governments within the Middle East might best be described as Democratic Islam. And by democracy here we mean more than just "one person, one vote." A number of countries in the Middle East, including Iran and Syria, have elections. Several years ago Egypt held free elections and the people elected a majority of candidates from the Muslim Brotherhood, which promptly began trying to implement its narrow vision of an Islamic state.

Democracy, in the Western sense, also includes the protection of personal rights and liberties, including freedom of religion, freedom of speech, freedom of the press, and freedom of assembly. By those standards the only consistent Islamic democracy in the Middle East has been Turkey. In 1928 Turkey amended its constitution and removed a statement that said the religion of the state was Islam. Its current constitution, adopted in 1982, prohibits discrimination on the basis of religious beliefs. The constitution also guarantees freedom of thought, freedom of the press, and the right to personal privacy. In many ways Turkey would seem to be the ideal model for Islamic democracy. However, things aren't always what they seem.

Former army officer Kemal Attatürk was the founder of the Republic of Turkey. He is the one who sought to pattern Turkey after the democracies of the West. And since its founding, the guardian of Turkey's secular values has been the military. On multiple occasions the military has stepped in to take over the government so that it wouldn't drift off course politically, economically, or religiously. Turkey's secular democracy was kept intact through the use of military coups . . . a very *undemocratic* process!

> In 1987 Turkey submitted its formal application to become a member of the European Economic Community, and by 1995 it was recognized as a candidate for full membership. But Europe had several concerns about Turkey's membership, and one was the military's "interference" in Turkey's political process. The armed forces pulled back . . . and the country started drifting away from secularism toward Islam.
>
> **Bernard Lewis**
> **"Islam and Liberal Democracy"**[7]

In 2002 the Islamist-based Justice and Development Party (known by its Turkish acronym AKP) won the national elections. The new prime minister was Recep Tayyip Erdoğan. In 2007 Abdullah Gül, a strong Islamist, announced his candidacy for the office of president. That office had historically been viewed as the guardian of Turkey's secular system, and the military saw Gül's candidacy as a direct assault by forces seeking to turn Turkey into an Islamic state. They issued a veiled warning, threatening another coup were he to win. Europe responded harshly. The European Union's Enlargement Commissioner said, "This is a clear test case whether the Turkish armed forces respect democratic secularization and democratic values."[8] The military backed down, and Gül was elected.

Since then the Turkish military, and Turkey's secular values, have been in retreat. The country continues to grow more openly Islamic, under an increasingly powerful leader. The "democratically elected government [of Turkey] is waging an all-out war against all rules and institutions of democracy. The newly enacted laws emphasize the survival of the party state at the expense of the rule of law and human rights."[9] When the US Foreign Relations Committee questioned Ambassador Designate John R. Bass during his confirmation hearing to serve as US Ambassador to Turkey, Senator John McCain questioned him on whether the administration was seeing a "drift toward authoritarianism" on the part of now-president Erdoğan. After some hesitancy, the Ambassador Designate admitted that there was "a drift in that direction."[10]

For nearly a century Turkey was the lone beacon of true Democratic Islam in the Middle East. But without military involvement to act as a counterweight, it appears that Turkey has begun a slide away from secularism toward a greater emphasis on Islam, all in the name of democracy.

AUTOCRATIC ISLAM

Autocratic Islam is the "catchall" category to describe several types of Islamic governments in the Middle East. The specific form of government varies, but they all share one thing in common—a government dominated by a strong leader. In some cases the government is a monarchy, as in Saudi Arabia or Jordan. In other cases it resembles a democracy, but with the leader kept in power by the military, as in Egypt or Syria. Autocratic Islam has actually been the most common type of government in the Middle East. Some leaders came to power by virtue of family lineage, while others seized power in a military coup. But from Muhammad, to Salah al-Din, to Gamal Abdel Nasser, to Hafez al-Assad, strong leaders have attracted followers—and enemies. And the leader's ability to reward his followers and defeat his enemies determined whether he would succeed or fail.

With so many different personalities, leadership styles, and forms of government, this category might seem too broad. But apart from having a strong leader, these governments also seem to share one other defining characteristic—Islam—as their own constitutions make clear:

- *Egypt.* "Islam is the religion of the State and Arabic is its official language. The principles of Islamic Sharia are the main source of legislation" (Article 2).
- *Iraq.* "Islam is the official religion of the State and it is a fundamental source of legislation" (Article 2).
- *Jordan.* "Islam is the religion of the State" (Article 2).
- *Saudi Arabia.* "In support of the Book of God and the Sunna of His Messenger . . . citizens shall give the pledge of allegiance to the King" (Article 6). "Government in the Kingdom of Saudi Arabia derives its authority from the Book of God and the Sunna of the Prophet . . . which are the ultimate sources of reference for this Law and the other laws of the State" (Article 7). "Governance in the Kingdom of Saudi Arabia is based on justice, shura [consultation] and equality according to Islamic Sharia" (Article 8).

- *Syria.* "The religion of the President of the Republic has to be Islam. . . . Islamic jurisprudence is a main source of legislation" (Article 3).

In these countries Islam isn't just the historical, cultural, or religious heritage of the state. It's part of the very fabric of the state itself. The West has sought to separate church and state as reflected in the US Constitution and the Bill of Rights. But in most Islamic countries, religion and state can't be separated.[11]

THEOCRATIC ISLAM

The final expression of Islamic government found in the Middle East would seem to be the purest, yet actually represents the most dangerous form: theocratic Islam. The term "theocratic" comes from two Greek words: *theos* ("God") and *cratos* ("rule"). A theocracy is God's direct rule over humanity. And if God is actually the One ruling, it should work perfectly. Unfortunately, that has rarely been the human experience under such human assumptions.

Within Islam, Shiite Iran might be viewed as the "model" of theocratic Islam. Though the country is officially a republic, the reality is that it is ruled by the ayatollahs. Ayatollah literally means "sign of God," and these rulers are viewed as God's visible presence on earth. They claim infallibility, so every decision they make is binding on their subjects. The Iranian constitution enshrines this theocracy into law when it states that "all civil, penal, financial, economic, administrative, cultural, military, political, and other laws and regulations must be based on Islamic criteria. This principle applies absolutely and generally to all articles of the Constitution as well as to all other laws and regulations, and the [wise persons] of the Guardian Council are judges in this matter."[12]

At the other end of the theological spectrum, though holding to a very similar style of leadership, is ISIS and its ruler, Abu Bakr al-Husayni al-Qurashi al-Baghdadi. Al-Baghdadi announced the reestablishment of an Islamic caliphate, with him in charge as Caliph Ibrahim. The word *caliph* comes from the Arabic word for succession and points back to a time when one individual ruled as the supreme religious and political leader. Al-Baghdadi is establishing a theocracy, and *he* will be the one speaking on behalf of God!

ISIS and Al-Qaeda are cut from the same theological cloth when it comes to establishing a caliphate. In its constitution, Al-Qaeda stated that its primary goal is "the victory of the mighty religion of Allah, the establishment of an Islamic Regime and the restoration of the Islamic Caliphate, God willing." The leadership of both groups expects absolute obedience from their followers. Al-Qaeda actually has its followers sign a contract, part of which says, "I swear allegiance to Allah, and with his accord to obey and listen to my superiors." This is more than just a legal requirement; it's also a religious duty. "The religious lawful duty, such as al-Jihad and the obedience to higher authorities, is every Muslim's duty by religious law."[13]

If ISIS and Al-Qaeda are so alike, why did ISIS step beyond Al-Qaeda and announce the formation of the caliphate? One possible reason might be the difference in family background and religious training between the leadership of the two groups. Al-Qaeda's founders were laymen—Osama bin Laden was an engineer and his replacement, Ayman al-Zawahiri, is a medical doctor. But Abu Bakr al-Baghdadi traces his family history back to the tribe of Muhammad. And in terms of theological training, "Baghdadi received his PhD from the Islamic University of Baghdad, with a focus on Islamic culture, history, sharia, and jurisprudence."[14]

THE RULE OF ISLAMIC GOVERNMENTS

Ayatollah Khomeini summarized his understanding of the "ideal" Islamic government, and it's a definition that seems to describe the governments of most Islamic states: "Islamic government is neither tyrannical nor absolute, but constitutional. It is not constitutional in the current sense of the word, i.e., based on the approval of laws in accordance with the opinion of the majority. It is constitutional in the sense that the rulers are subject to a certain set of conditions in governing and administering the country, conditions that are set forth in the [Qur'an] and *Sunnah* (traditions of the prophets). . . . [It can be described] as the rule of divine law over men."[15]

In the Middle East it doesn't really matter what "variety" of government is in control. Whatever skin might cover the outside, the bones, muscles, sinews, and organs that give it life are Islam and the Quran. And if knowledge is power, then men like al-Baghdadi are indeed powerful, because they have the ability to use the Quran to conjure up images of past glory and, at whatever violent cost, all future conquest.

7

OIL AND WATER: SEEING THE BIGGER PICTURE

The beginning of understanding is to appreciate that resolving this situation is immensely complex.

TONY BLAIR
Former British Prime Minister[1]

Sectarian violence racks the Middle East, and ethnic differences compound the problem. A visit to Samarra, Iraq, might just help us understand more fully why. So take hold of the inside railing and journey to the top of the Malwiya Minaret at the ruins of the Great Mosque of Samarra.

The minaret's name, *Malwiya*, comes from the Arabic word for *twisted*. And the 170-foot climb to the top of the spiral stairway, without any outside guardrail, is a dizzying adventure. (See opposite page.) The minaret was built nearly thirteen hundred years ago and provides a spectacular view of this city along the Tigris River some seventy miles north of Baghdad.

From this bird's-eye view, we gain the perspective needed to appreciate and understand the complexity that causes so much of the difficulty in the Middle East today.

These ruins below us are the remains of the Great Mosque of Samarra. And the golden dome in the distance is the al-Askari Mosque. (See picture on opposite page.) Recent events have not been kind to Samarra. The top of the Malwiya Minaret from where this picture was taken was partially destroyed by a bomb in 2005. The al-Askari Mosque was blown up by Sunni insurgents in 2006, and its two minarets were destroyed in 2007!

ANCIENT RUINS, MODERN SIGNIFICANCE

Yet Samarra's significance runs much deeper. The city was founded in AD 836 by an Abbasid caliph who moved his capital here from Baghdad. For fifty years Samarra ruled the Islamic world until a later caliph moved the capital back to Baghdad. The al-Askari Mosque contains the mausoleums of the tenth and eleventh Shiite Imams, and Samarra was the place where the twelfth and final Imam (the Mahdi) went into hiding. That makes the al-Askari Mosque one of the holiest sites for Shiites. Yet most inhabitants of Samarra are Sunnis. The city is part of the "Sunni triangle," that region in Iraq where most Sunni Arabs live.

The people of Samarra endured a major international conflict in the eighteenth century. The Battle of Samarra in 1733 would decide the fate of the entire region. In that monumental nine-hour struggle, seventy thousand Persians fought against eighty thousand Ottomans. The Ottomans almost lost the battle when two thousand Kurds in their army fled.

But the Ottomans held on to defeat the Persian army, break the siege of Baghdad, and retain control of the region. That victory, however, came at a steep price. By the end of the day, fifty thousand soldiers from the two sides had been killed or wounded.

Now imagine growing up in Samarra. Playing in the ruins of what was once the capital of an Islamic caliphate. Experiencing firsthand the religious tensions between the Sunnis and Shiites. Learning of battles fought between the major ethnic and religious forces of the day for control of the region. While others from Samarra might have dreamed about the town's glorious past, one hometown boy has used that history to reshape Islam's future. His name is Abu Bakr al-Baghdadi —the founder and self-proclaimed caliph of ISIS!

THE ARABS: CAMELOT . . . OR CAMEL LOT?

The West struggles to understand how a group as brutal as ISIS—and its determined leader Abu Bakr—could rise so quickly and be so successful. What Western nations have failed to grasp is that the Middle East is locked in a struggle involving four volatile issues: oil, water, religion, and ethnicity. We've explored the religious issues, but to understand the ISIS crisis we need a clearer understanding of the other three. So let's take a tour of the ethnic groups that dominate the region to see how they intersect with ISIS.

The Middle East was an enigma to most Americans until the early twentieth century. An American naval officer and historian coined the term "Middle East" in 1902 to describe the area in the middle of Arabia and India.[2] The region had been under the control of the Ottoman Empire for almost four centuries.

Much of the Arabian Peninsula was the province of Hejaz, while what is today called Iraq was divided along religious and ethnic lines into the provinces of Basra, Baghdad, and Mosul. The province of Syria controlled much of modern-day Syria and Jordan, while the province of Beirut controlled what is today Lebanon, northwest Syria, and northern Israel. Jerusalem was its own separate region.[3]

By the end of the nineteenth century, Western travelers were beginning to visit the Middle East. But those Americans who came, and who then wrote about their travels, focused on the unique, the strange, and the unusual. Much like visitors to England describing castles, those who journeyed to the Middle East were more apt to describe their first encounter with a camel.[4] Others wrote about quaint, or hostile, natives. In his popular travel guide on *Palestine and Syria*, Karl Baedeker even issued his own personal travel warnings for certain towns. "It is advisable [in Hebron] to take a Guide . . . as the Moslems here are notorious for their fanaticism. Travellers are earnestly warned against that arrant beggar, the son of the deceased old sheikh Hamza."⁵

The fascination and confusion about the Middle East only intensified over time.

All the way up until World War I the West didn't grasp the complexity of this ancient and unique part of the world. Americans focused on the religious, searching out connections to the events and stories in the Bible.⁶ Meanwhile, Europe's focus was more economic. The European powers had colonized the New World, Africa, and the Far East. Now with the decline of the Ottoman Empire they saw an opportunity to do the same thing in the Middle East.⁷

But if Europe saw the Middle East as an opportunity for colonial expansion, those living in the Middle East saw Europe as their gateway to freedom from Ottoman control. The majority of those living in the Middle East were Arabic-speaking, Sunni Muslims. While they didn't really embrace nationalism, there was a sense of tribal or ethnic identity along with a strong religious connection to the region. And they *did* chafe under the rule of the Ottomans.

The leader of the self-proclaimed kingdom of the Hejaz was the sharif and emir of Mecca, Ali bin Hussein. He began the Arab revolt against the Ottoman Empire and appointed himself as the first king of the Arabs and eventually as caliph. Unfortunately, his claim didn't go unchallenged. The Saudi clan rejected his authority and eventually drove him out of the Arabian Peninsula. Whatever hope there had been of Arab unity dissolved as the different tribes and regions couldn't agree on a leader they could all follow.

Arab nationalism itself is nothing more than the conviction that the Arabs constitute one great historical nation, divided only by a series of imperial overlords, from the Mongols through the Ottomans up to the Western powers, most recently the United States and Israel. The destiny of the Arabs then is to reunite and thereby overcome the divisions, and borders, forced on them by foreigners.

Lee Smith
"Iraqi Insurgents Boast They're Building an Arab Super-State" [8]

But the vision didn't die. For the past century the Arab world dreamed of an Arab state, a single entity under which all Arabs could unite. Gamal Abdel Nasser of Egypt sought to promote his vision of Arab nationalism that would oppose all colonialism (which, to him, included the state of Israel) and would create in its place a unified pan-Arab state.

Nasser's plan failed, but it was followed by the rise of the Ba'ath parties in Syria and Iraq—led respectively by Hafez al-Assad and Saddam Hussein. The philosophy and goals in both countries were the same, though the religious orientation of the leaders differed. "Saddam Hussein thinks in terms of circles," said Haifa University professor Amitzia Baram. "His most immediate circle is the gulf, which remains No. 1 for him. But beyond that there is the circle of the Arab world, where he aspires to hegemony."[9]

Hussein desired total dominance over the region. But the Ba'athist philosophy couldn't even unite the two countries that claimed it as their own.

And yet, the concept of pan-Arab unity remains an idea that just won't die. A leading Arab member of Israel's Knesset (parliament) caused a firestorm when he voiced the same sentiments in 2014. "We support one united state in the Arab world as preparation for one united state in the entire Islamic world of 1.4 billion people . . . . I want a civilian state that will operate according to the path of the prophets and caliphates that go on the upright path."[10]

The siren song of Arab unity has been sounding for the past century, and it has attracted a number of leaders, with disastrous consequences for all. ISIS is the latest in a string of would-be caliphs seeking to unite all Sunni Arabs—and eventually all Muslims—into a single Islamic state.

IRAN: PERSIA IN SEARCH OF AN EMPIRE

To most Americans, Iran remains an enigma. In 1979 Iran and the United States broke off diplomatic relations following the rise of the Islamic Republic and the seizure of the US embassy in Tehran. Eventually, Iran joined an elite club in US foreign policy—one of three nations identified as part of an "axis of evil" by President George W. Bush. So what is it about Iran that makes it so unique? Again, the answer lies tucked away in the past.

Adolf Hitler talked about the superiority of the "Aryan master race." But before the Nazis hijacked that word, Aryan wasn't used to describe racial superiority. It simply referred to those who shared a common Indo-European heritage. And one of those Aryan countries was Iran. In fact, the name "Iran" comes from the same root as *Aryan*, meaning "noble ones."

> Iran aggressively pursues these weapons [of mass destruction] and exports terror. . . . States like these, and their terrorist allies, constitute an axis of evil, arming to threaten the peace of the world.
>
> **President George W. Bush**
> **State of the Union Address,**
> **January 29, 2002**

The terms "Iran" and "Persia" are often used interchangeably. And while they are not totally identical, they do overlap.

Ancient Persia occupied a large portion of what is today modern Iran. And the official language spoken in Iran is Farsi, which is just a modern version of Old Persian, now written with an Arabic script. Iranians are *not* Arabs, they *don't* speak Arabic, and the vast majority are not Sunni Muslims. And historically, they have always tried to expand their empire westward.

A JEWISH PROPHET FORETELLS PERSIA'S FUTURE

In the Old Testament book of Daniel, the prophet had a vision where he stood at the citadel of Susa in what is now southwestern Iran. In the vision he saw a two-horned ram "butting westward, northward, and southward, and no other beasts could stand before him nor was there anyone to rescue from his power, but he did as he pleased and magnified himself" (Daniel 8:4). The angel Gabriel then offered Daniel an explanation. "The ram which you saw with the two horns represents the kings of Media and Persia" (Daniel 8:20).

Daniel lived long enough to see the initial fulfillment of the vision. Cyrus, king of the Medo-Persian Empire, moved his army westward and captured all of Babylonia. Eventually the Persians expanded southward to Egypt and northward to Asia Minor (modern Turkey). Their advance was finally halted, and reversed, by the Greeks. But for two hundred years the Persians ruled the Middle East.

After the rise of Alexander the Great, the Middle East turned its gaze westward, as Greece and then Rome dominated the Mediterranean Basin. But another power rose in Iran to replace the Medo-Persian Empire. The Parthians, from northeastern Iran, eventually built an empire that stretched from the Euphrates River on the west to the Indus River on the east. And the battleground between Parthia and Rome ran right through the Middle East.

Less than fifty years before the birth of Jesus, the two superpowers fought a battle in what is today southeastern Turkey. The Parthians defeated the Romans, killing twenty thousand soldiers and capturing an additional ten thousand, in one of Rome's worst military defeats. Two decades later the Parthians attacked Judea, forcing Herod the Great to flee Jerusalem, leave his family at Masada, and take a circuitous route to solicit Rome for help regaining his throne.

CONFLICT IN THE ISLAMIC PERIOD

In the early Islamic period the Muslim Arabs fought a major battle against the Persians. That battle, in AD 636, is known as the Battle of Qadisiyya. And the Muslim Arabs won. For a time they were the masters. But a Persian revival occurred. Iran "was indeed Islamized, but it was not Arabized. Persians remained Persians."[11]

Whether it was the difference in language or ethnicity, the Persians remained distinct. And that distinction soon involved Islam itself.

A new dynasty developed around the Caspian Sea that eventually controlled all of what is now Iran. It was the Safavid Dynasty, and its first ruler was Shah Ismail I. One of the most influential decisions he made was to adopt Shiite Islam as the official religion of his kingdom. The Safavid Dynasty only lasted for two centuries, but it played a key role in unifying Persia under a common language and a common Shiite religion. Both set Persia, now Iran, in direct opposition to the Arabic-speaking Sunnis to the west.

CONFLICT IN THE LATE TWENTIETH CENTURY

Fast-forward to 1979, when Ayatollah Khomeini and the Iranian revolution overthrew the final Shah of Iran in 1979. It now seemed conflict with the Arabs was inevitable. Khomeini made no secret of his dislike of the surrounding Arab nations and their dependence on the West. And he telegraphed his intention to export his Shiite brand of Islamic fundamentalism to the Shiite minorities in these other countries.

Once again the Persians were looking to expand their kingdom.

The same year that Ayatollah Khomeini took control of Iran, Saddam Hussein seized power in Iraq and inaugurated his long, violent, and iron-fisted rule. One year later, in 1980, Hussein invaded Iran to start the eight-year Iran–Iraq War. That was also the year he started rebuilding ancient Babylon. The connection was lost on the West, but not on those living in the Middle East. This could not have been a bolder, clearer statement of the "grandeur of the Iraqis to pursue their path for more glories," as the Iraqi Minister of Information and Culture would later proclaim.[12]

The Iran–Iraq War is history, and so are Saddam Hussein and Ayatollah Khomeini. But the Arab nations' fear of Shiite-led Iran continues. Iran has become a radical military and religious state, only intensifying the Sunni-Shiite tensions.[13] The whole region is on edge because of Iran's increasing nuclear threat. A satellite photo released in 2013 showed launchpads for Saudi missiles pointing at two cities—Tel Aviv and Tehran. The launchpad toward Israel was expected, the one toward Tehran was not. The head of the Institute for Air and Space Strategic Studies concluded that "the intended recipient of Saudi Arabia's missile warnings is Iran."[14]

After the fall of Saddam Hussein, Iraq's Shiite majority took control . . . with America's help. And their old enemy Iran soon replaced the United States as their new sponsor and helper. ISIS received support from Iraq's Sunni population because, in large measure, they felt disenfranchised and threatened by the Iranian-backed Shiite government of Nouri al-Malaki.

TURKEY, WHERE WATER IS LIFE

The Ottoman Empire began in Turkey. Eventually it would expand to control most of the Middle East, and part of southeastern Europe. When the Turkish forces captured Constantinople in 1453, they assumed control over the Byzantine Empire. And until their defeat in World War I, the Ottoman Empire dominated the Middle East as Islam's last caliphate. To many of the Arabs in the Middle East, Turkey poses an imminent, existential threat because it controls the water of the Tigris and Euphrates Rivers.

And in the Middle East, water is life.

Beginning in the 1970s, Turkey started constructing twenty-two dams and nineteen hydroelectric power plants on the Tigris and Euphrates Rivers. The water resources and electricity have helped Turkey modernize and develop. But Turkey's progress has come at a steep price for Syria and Iraq, the two countries downstream. In fact, according to one 2012 report, "one projection states that, when completed, [the project] will reduce the flow of water into Iraq by approximately 80 percent and into Syria by about 40 percent."[15]

The reduced flow in water is a problem, but two factors have turned that problem into a crisis. The first is Syria's and Iraq's growing population. In 1980 Syria had just under nine million citizens. By 2013 the number had swelled to nearly twenty-three million, a 150 percent increase. During that same period, Iraq's population more than doubled, increasing from just under fourteen million to over thirty-three million. More people needing water, with less flowing down the two main rivers, lays the groundwork for intense and long-standing conflict.

> The outcome of the Iraq and Syrian conflicts may rest on who controls the region's dwindling water supplies.
>
> **John Vidal**
> *The Guardian*[16]

The reduced flow on the Tigris and Euphrates Rivers has been compounded even more by a second problem—a prolonged drought. In 2014 an environmental economist framed the problem in catastrophic terms, describing a sustained drought not seen in over a century.[17]

More people trying to survive on less water. Farmland shriveling under the hot Middle Eastern sun. No water for irrigation. All of it provides the making of a vulnerable state in need of a unifying force.

THE KURDS: THE LARGEST MINORITY WITHOUT A COUNTRY

The final ethnic group intersecting with other groups in the Middle East is the Kurds. With a population approaching thirty million, the Kurds are the largest ethnic group in the world without their own country.[18] The Kurdish people currently reside in a region that spans four countries—Iran, Iraq, Syria, and Turkey. And they have battled with each of these countries for the right of self-determination.

The origin of the Kurds isn't completely understood. They inhabit the region that was once home to the ancient Medes, but not everyone believes the two groups are related. However, the Kurds and Medes do share one historical reality. Both have been overshadowed by their neighbors. The Medes were the lesser half of the Medo-Persian Empire; and today's Kurds are controlled by Turks, Arabs, and Persians who are opposed to having the Kurds form their own country.

For over thirty years the Kurds have fought against these governments to establish an independent country of Kurdistan. In 1988, at the end of the Iran–Iraq War, Saddam Hussein launched an attack against the restive Kurds living in northern Iraq. As many as two hundred thousand Kurds were killed in that campaign. Iran killed nearly thirty thousand Kurds putting down the insurgency in their country. Turkey killed an estimated thirty-five thousand Kurds, destroyed four thousand villages, and displaced up to a million refugees in their fight against the Kurds. Syria's opposition to the Kurds had been less volatile, but that started to change with the rise of ISIS.

When ISIS first moved into northern Iraq, the Kurds chose not to intervene. The Kurds and ISIS were both Sunnis. And both disliked the Shiite-dominated government in Baghdad. But, as a Kurdish politician now admits, "The policy of indifference with regard to the ISIS attack on Iraq was a mistake."[19]

Why did ISIS ultimately turn on the Kurds? Ethnic differences and the unwillingness of the Kurds to submit to ISIS's harsh interpretation of the Quran were two major reasons. But there was a third reason—oil. The Kurds in northern Iraq control several oil fields, and ISIS is desperate for revenue to continue its advances.

ISIS SUCCESS AMID MIDDLE EAST UNREST

The success of ISIS is due, in part, to larger issues roiling the Middle East. Iran's support for the Shiite-dominated government in Iraq is based on religious affinity, but it has left the Sunnis in Iraq feeling disenfranchised and threatened. Turkey's hoarding of water has also created economic hardship and increased ethnic tensions. For the Sunnis in Syria and Iraq, ISIS appeared onstage at just the right time, offering help and hope. Unless the economic or political landscape changes dramatically, ISIS seems to have home field advantage.

For most people, oil and water don't mix. For ISIS, oil and water represent everything. And they're determined to control both in order to control everything.

8

WILL ISIS LEAD TO ARMAGEDDON?

You will be hearing of wars and rumors of wars. See that you are not frightened, for those things must take place, but that is not yet the end.

JESUS
Matthew 24:6

D evelopments around the Middle East suggest America's campaign against ISIS might actually be helping, rather than hurting, the organization. In a message to his followers, the caliph of ISIS boasted of the group's ever-growing support. "We announce to you the expansion of the Islamic State to new countries, to the countries of the Haramayn [Saudi Arabia], Yemen, Egypt, Libya, Algeria."[1] So far, Islamic groups in at least ten countries have pledged their support to ISIS.[2]

If ISIS were a corporation, we might describe it as being actively engaged in signing up franchisees. But a better comparison might be to that of a dictator looking for allies—and offering them a share of the spoil in return for their allegiance.

ISIS has been relentless in pursuing its goal. In the process, it has become a well-organized, well-funded terror organization. In fact, most recently, ISIS has begun a sophisticated recruitment campaign, hoping to attract engineers and executives to assist them in operating their newfound oil empire—all of which has emerged from captured oil-rich territories across Iran and Syria.[3] But what happens next?

SETTING THE STAGE FOR FUTURE THINGS

Abu Musa, a spokesman for ISIS, made a brash claim about its future goals. "We will humiliate [America] everywhere, God willing, and we will raise the flag of Allah in the White House."[4] Is he delusional or discerning? Does ISIS have the ability to continue expanding, or will its collapse be as sudden and dramatic as its rise? And, perhaps most significantly, does its rise to prominence have any prophetic significance?

Both the Bible and Islam speak often about the future. And the parallels between the two are, at times, remarkable. In his book *The Islamic Antichrist*, Joel Richardson identifies twenty-two specific similarities.[5] But do these similarities suggest a biblical and prophetic destiny for Islam or could there be other reasons for the parallels?

Richardson has done a remarkable job describing Islam and presenting the parallels between Islam and the future Antichrist. But there are strong reasons from the Bible to believe ISIS isn't on the pathway to Armageddon. The parallels between what the Bible and Islam say about the future can be explained, in part, by the fact that Muhammad drew much of his teaching from the Old and New Testament Scriptures. He tried to incorporate Jewish and Christian teachings into Islam, which he claimed to be the final revelation. So it shouldn't be surprising that the Quran contains references to the Messiah, the return of Jesus, a final gathering of nations, or even a cataclysmic final battle.

When looking at Islam's view of the future, it is important to remember the difference between something that is original and something that is an imperfect copy. The Old and New Testament Scriptures harmonize in a way that provides an accurate description of events leading up to the return of Jesus and the establishment of God's kingdom on earth. They don't tell us everything, but all that they do tell us is true. Muhammad borrowed from the Bible to paint his personal vision of the future. But rather than synchronizing with the Bible, his vision of the future in the Quran becomes more a distortion of biblical teaching.

> Muslims await a man who will claim to be Jesus Christ.... The biblical description of the False Prophet and the Islamic description of the Muslim Jesus on all the essential points are identical.
>
> **Joel Richardson**
> *The Islamic Antichrist*[6]

Someone viewing Picasso's *Seated Woman* can indeed see that it is a painting of a woman sitting in chair. But her face is blue, her hair is green, and her eyes are misplaced on her face. Trying to identify the real subject of the work from the painting is virtually impossible. The image is just too distorted. And that's also true of the Quran's perspective on the future. It has similarities to the Bible, but most are superficial.

ISIS is looking for the Islamic Mahdi. And some see comparisons between the Mahdi and the rise of the biblical Antichrist. But could the Antichrist ever come from an Islamic group like ISIS? It's very unlikely for three reasons.

SIGNS OF THE ANTICHRIST: HE WILL HAVE THE TRUST OF ISRAEL

The biblical book of Daniel records a remarkable prophecy spanning 490 years of history (Daniel 9:24–27). Most of that prophecy has been fulfilled (483 years), but one final seven-year period remains unfulfilled. Jesus referred to the prophecy as He described the future events that will lead up to His return (Matthew 24:15). And in the New Testament book of Revelation, John reaffirmed the exact timing for the second half of this final seven-year period (Revelation 11:2–3; 13:5). But what many overlook when studying Daniel 9 is its unique focus on the Jewish people and Jerusalem. The prophecy was given in response to Daniel's prayer for the city of Jerusalem and for his people (Daniel 9:16–19). When the angel Gabriel arrived with God's answer, he announced that the prophecy involved "your people and your holy city" (v. 24).[7]

The final seven-year tribulation period begins when the Antichrist makes "a firm covenant with the many for one week" (Daniel 9:27). Since the focus of Daniel's prayer—and God's answer—is on Israel, the covenant that begins this final time must somehow be connected to the Jewish people. And when the person making the covenant breaks it in the middle of the seven-year period, it must be Israel whom he is betraying.

Why is Daniel's focus on Jerusalem and the Jewish people so important? If the covenant being made is between the Antichrist and Israel, then it is very difficult to envision an Islamic Antichrist. Would Israel ever place its trust in an Islamic ruler for the country's national security? That notion is highly unlikely. The events of the past seven decades have given Israel little incentive to trust their Muslim neighbors. And if this future leader is a devout follower of Islam, Israel would be even less trusting.

SIGNS OF THE ANTICHRIST: HE IS WELCOMED BY THE WORLD

The apostle John describes the time when the Antichrist first appears on the world stage. "I looked, and behold, a white horse, and he who sat on it had a bow; and a crown was given to him, and he went out conquering and to conquer" (Revelation 6:2). By describing the Antichrist riding onto the world stage on a white horse, John is picturing him as a conquering hero. Later Jesus, the true Christ, will also appear on a white horse, John writes, when He returns to earth at the end of the tribulation period (Revelation 19:11).

A weary world will welcome this leader and Antichrist as someone who will finally resolve its many problems and bring peace. The apostle Paul describes the start of this tribulation period as a time when people will be saying "Peace and safety!" (1 Thessalonians 5:3). When the Antichrist arrives, he will offer Israel and the world global peace. Many will trust him because of his promise of safety and security.

It's hard to imagine the rest of the world viewing the arrival of an Islamic Antichrist, especially of the brand of ISIS, with any sense of peace and safety. Our reaction to the rise of ISIS has been just the opposite. Neither Israel nor the West find comfort in Islamic conquests accompanied by such barbaric strategies and impulses.

SIGNS OF THE ANTICHRIST: HE ARISES FROM THE ROMAN EMPIRE

The prophet Daniel gave several clues that help identify the Antichrist. In Daniel 2 and 7 he identified four specific world powers that would arise in succession and exert control over the Promised Land until the coming of the Messiah. They were Babylon, Medo-Persia, Greece, and Rome. When Jesus appeared at His first coming, Rome was indeed in control.

But in both chapters the final predictions about the Roman Empire are yet to be fulfilled. The statue in chapter 2 hasn't yet been smashed, nor does God's kingdom yet control the earth. And the fourth beast's final three-and-a-half year time of terror in chapter 7 hasn't yet taken place. The Roman Empire was here at Christ's first coming, and a revived form of that empire needs to be here at the time of His return.

Daniel provides a second clue to help identify the Antichrist. In Daniel 9:27 he describes the future seven-year time of trouble for Israel. It begins when "he" establishes a covenant. But who is "he"? We need to look back at the previous verse for the antecedent. In Daniel 9:26 it is revealed that following the death of the Messiah "the people of the prince who is to come will destroy the city and the sanctuary." This coming "prince" is the Antichrist. And we can know his identity, in part, because his people were the ones who destroyed Jerusalem and the temple after Christ's death. The Romans did just that in AD 70.

The Roman Empire controlled a large swath of territory. In fact, the Roman Empire ringed the Mediterranean Basin. While some of that region is today Islamic, the core of the Roman Empire—Italy and the region in Europe—is not.

DOES ISIS FIT INTO BIBLE PROPHECY?

So where does ISIS fit in the prophetic timeline? The best answer seems to be that it doesn't. Could God be using ISIS to reshape the Middle East? Indeed that is possible. God has worked throughout history, causing nations to rise and fall as He controls world events. And ISIS is under God's control.

But while everyone is focusing on ISIS, another danger looms just over the horizon. And this threat *will* play a role in God's end-time drama.

ISIS ECLIPSED: THE ULTIMATE ISLAMIC THREAT

As I went around and met with people in the course of our discussions about the ISIL [Islamic State] coalition . . . there wasn't a leader I met within the region who didn't raise with me spontaneously the need to try to get peace between Israel and the Palestinians, because it was a cause of recruitment and of street anger and agitation that they felt.

JOHN KERRY
Secretary of State[1]

P eace has always been a rare commodity in the Middle East. And yet, the Bible describes a day when Israel will apparently be at peace with her neighbors. But will a formal agreement between Israel and the Palestinians lead to peace in the rest of the Middle East? Will it cause Islamic fundamentalism's hatred for Israel to vanish?

Sadly, it will not. Any Israeli–Palestinian peace will require the Palestinians to acknowledge Israel's right to exist

> In the latter years you will come into the land that is restored from the sword, whose inhabitants have been gathered from many nations to the mountains of Israel . . . its people were brought out from the nations, and they are living securely, all of them. You will go up, you will come like a storm; you will be like a cloud covering the land, you and all your troops, and many peoples with you.
>
> **Ezekiel 38:8–9**

as a Jewish state. And that is something many Islamic fundamentalists will never accept. ISIS might not survive, but later a far more powerful, and deadly, coalition will eclipse it.

The prophet Ezekiel describes a time when that coalition will launch an attack against Israel. Another army will someday surge across the Middle East. They won't be carrying the black flags of ISIS, but their intent will be just as evil and destructive. And they will appear, at least at first, to achieve far more than ISIS could ever have imagined.

THE NON-ISLAMIC COALITION LEADER AND THE COUNTRY HE RULES

In Ezekiel 38, the prophet describes a coalition of nations that will attack Israel at a time when the country finally seems to be at peace. The nations that Ezekiel identified don't appear on modern maps—Magog, Meshech, Tubal, Persia, Cush, Put, Gomer, and Beth-togarmah. But they were real countries in Ezekiel's day. Some are mentioned as early as Genesis 10. But where would we travel today to find these ancient lands . . . and who is their mysterious leader, the man named "Gog"?

About Gog. Ezekiel begins by identifying the leader of this future coalition. The man named Gog is from the land of Magog (Ezekiel 38:1). And that's the place where many quietly close their Bibles and back away! But there are some details that can help us identify this man and the country he rules. The first detail happens to be his name.

Many believe that the name "Gog" is equivalent to king Gyges, who ruled the kingdom of Lydia. Gyges grew up in what is now northeastern Turkey. Several different legends exist of how he rose to power, but they all agree that he seized control of the kingdom by killing the king and marrying his widow. Gyges spent the rest of his life expanding his kingdom, eventually dying in battle. While the exact date of his death is disputed, he apparently died less than a century before Ezekiel made his prediction.

But if Gyges was already dead, why would Ezekiel predict that Gog/Gyges would lead an invasion of Israel "in the latter years" (Ezekiel 38:8)? Leslie Allen offers an intriguing suggestion. "As with the national names, so here a great figure of the past is evidently used to define a future threat, as we might speak fearfully of a new Hitler."[2] Gyges had been a ruthless ruler who pushed to expand his empire. And living as he did just before the time of Ezekiel, he represented to that generation the most fearsome threat ever to have come from the far north.

By identifying a future leader as Gog/Gyges, Ezekiel paints a one-word picture of a ruthless man willing to eliminate anyone, or anything, standing in his way. He was the ancient equivalent of Hitler . . . or Stalin . . . or Al-Baghdadi!

It's also possible that Ezekiel identifies this leader as Gog because of a powerful word association. Cooper suggests the word Gog comes from the Sumerian word *gug*, which means "darkness."[3] In a very frightening way this future ruler will act as a human eclipse, casting his shadow across the Middle East. It's an appropriate description of this coming evil leader.

About Magog. Gog might be the ruler, but where exactly is the land of Magog over which he rules? Many in the past identified Magog with the Scythians who occupied the region north of the Black Sea in what is today Ukraine and Russia. The Scythians were actually nomadic tribesmen, and it's possible that Magog referred to a specific group or region among the Scythians. But find the Black Sea on a map and look to the north. That's the land of Magog.

About Meshech and Tubal. Gog is also "the chief prince" (38:3 NIV)[4] of Meshech and Tubal. These countries were in the region of ancient Cappadocia in what is today northeastern Anatolia. "The geographical area would today include parts of Iran, Turkey, and southern provinces of Russia."[5]

THE ULTIMATE ISLAMIC COALITION

Persia, Cush, and Put. The next three nations listed by Ezekiel (v. 5) are nations allied with Gog—all nations invited to join with him in the invasion. And all three countries have modern-day equivalents. The Persians came from the area that is today Iran. Cush was the region south of Egypt. While some translations identify it as Ethiopia, it also includes Sudan. And Put referred to the people west of Egypt who today make up the country of Libya. So joining Gog are three allies, all from different points of the compass. Israel had faced enemies from the north, east, south, and west before. But in this future invasion the enemies come from the extremes of the compass, at least from Israel's perspective.

Gomer and Beth-togarmah. Ezekiel included two final allies, his compass circling around to point once again toward the north. Gomer is identified with the ancient Cimmerians, and the "house of Togarmah" with the region around Armenia.

ISIS ECLIPSED: THE ULTIMATE ISLAMIC THREAT

Both started in the region of the Black and Caspian Seas and eventually pushed their way into the Anatolian peninsula.[6] Togarmah has also been identified with the Turks or Turkic peoples, one of several groups of nomadic peoples that migrated into this region.[7]

ARRANGING THE PROPHETIC PIECES

Ezekiel's vision provides an amazing profile of a coalition that has not yet existed on earth. The leader is an empire builder who resembles a ruthless ruler known in Ezekiel's day as Gyges —a sort of Hitler-like figure of that future generation.

But lest we wonder where he is really from, Ezekiel identifies him as the one ruling a region north of the Black Sea, though his empire extends down into the area between the Black and Caspian Seas. He is specifically said to be from "the remote parts of the north" (v. 15).

This new and ruthless leader will assemble a patchwork of countries into an invasion force, the likes of which the modern world has never known. Moving clockwise around the Near East, Ezekiel identifies the allies by region. Today the countries occupying those regions are Iran, Sudan, Libya, and Turkey.

The Forecast Allies of Gog

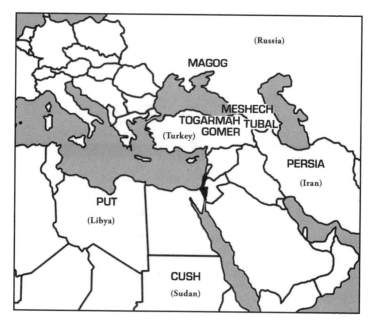

As we place these ancient nations and groups on a contemporary map, we make an interesting discovery: All the allies of Gog match up with areas that today are either dominated by Islamic fundamentalism or struggling with its factions. Iran became an Islamic state under Ayatollah Khomeini. The northern half of Sudan harbored bin Laden for a time, and is the country that has served as an arms transport base for funneling weapons from Iran to Hamas terrorists. Libya has disintegrated into warring Islamic factions, yet continues to supply fighters and weapons to ISIS and to Islamic forces in Egypt and Gaza. Turkey is officially a secular country, but the party in power has its roots in Islamic fundamentalism. Visions of Turkish imperialism, and a revived Ottoman Empire, seem to lie just below the surface.

But these different countries aren't natural allies. Sunnis dominate in Turkey, Libya, and Sudan, while Shiites maintain control of Iran. Libya and Sudan are Arabic; Iran and Turkey are not. These nations have different languages and different cultures. On the surface they have little in common.

Ezekiel's prophecy, however, suggests two factors will enable them to overcome these differences—a common hatred for Israel and an overwhelming desire for material gain. The leader from the north will use these desires to forge together an army sharing mutual interests and mutual goals.

There might also be a third element motivating Gog's allies. As discussed earlier, both branches of Islam believe in a final world battle where the Jews will be destroyed and the Islamic Messiah revealed. Perhaps some will join in this invasion in the belief that the attack will hasten the coming of the end and thus bring ultimate victory for the followers of Allah and the coming of their Messiah.

THE DARKER MOTIVE

Ezekiel identifies Gog's primary motive for the invasion. He will come "to capture spoil and to seize plunder" (Ezekiel 38:12). Gog's purpose for invading is primarily economic.

Something in the land of Israel will give this leader a compelling economic reason to invade. Ezekiel doesn't say what it is, but the answer might sit underneath the Mediterranean Sea—enormous reserves of oil and natural gas.

Energy fuels much of the current crisis in the Middle East, often in ways we don't fully understand. Russia supplies Europe with natural gas, and on occasion has leveraged that energy source as a diplomatic weapon. Russia has also worked hard to keep other suppliers from cutting into its near-monopoly.

A proposed pipeline to bring natural gas from Qatar to Europe, through Syria and Turkey, was rejected by Syria—a cozy but troublesome Russian ally. "No doubt this refusal provided an additional impetus to Qatar and Turkey for the sake of moving forward in supporting the Syrian revolutionaries financially and militarily."[8]

Alternative sources of oil and natural gas—and the ability to transport those sources—are two variables that concern Russia. Could Israel's energy independence—already demonstrated in its proposal to transport excess natural gas supplies to the European continent[9]—be perceived as a threat to the current status quo? Could a peace treaty between Israel and the surrounding countries provide an opportunity for countries like Qatar to run an alternative pipeline through Israel that would bypass Syria, Turkey, and Russia altogether? These are all significant possibilities and pose a real and present threat to powerful, energy-hungry empires to the north.

Control over the energy wealth of Israel—and any facilities built to transport that energy abroad—might well be sufficient motivation for Gog and his allies to invade.

Ezekiel provides one additional hint as to the purpose for this invasion. In Ezekiel 38:13 two groups express alarm over the threatened invasion. "Sheba and Dedan and the merchants of Tarshish" ask the invaders if they are coming to plunder them. So who are these countries, and how do they help us identify the purpose for the attack?

Sheba and Dedan were in the present-day Arabian Peninsula. Sheba was at the very southern end of the peninsula, in the region of modern Yemen. Dedan was farther north, in what is today Saudi Arabia. About a century before Ezekiel's prophecy, Isaiah also wrote about Dedan (Isaiah 21:13) and Sheba (60:6).

Isaiah specifically connected Dedan with "Arabia" and describes the "caravans of Dedanites," suggesting the place was known for its nomadic traders who used camels. He also described Sheba as a place with a "multitude of camels."

Ezekiel's use of Tarshish is a little more thorny to navigate. Most assume Tarshish is a place in the far western Mediterranean—like Spain. But why would a region that far to the west be worried about an attack in the east? Ezekiel doesn't say Tarshish is worried about the impending attack; he says the "the merchants of Tarshish" are the ones concerned. These "merchants" are traders *from* the west (Tarshish). Dedan and Sheba are from the eastern desert and the "merchants of Tarshish" came from the western Mediterranean. Both are wealthy and both are afraid they might be the objects of the impending attack.

The army of Gog and his allies are coming to attack Israel. His goal is to seize and plunder Israel's wealth. But, at least initially, the final objective of the attack isn't completely clear. That's why these other groups are nervous. They ask, in effect, "You aren't coming to attack us, are you?"

So how might such a scenario look today? Imagine Russia assembling an army that includes elements from Iran, Sudan, Libya, and Turkey. It becomes clear they are heading toward the central part of the Middle East. But they haven't yet telegraphed their final destination. Saudi Arabia is worried the army might be coming to take control of its oil fields. (Russia would be helping out two of Saudi Arabia's main rivals—Turkey and Iran.)

Meanwhile western merchants are also nervous that the army might be coming to seize the Suez Canal and block the trade route on which they are so dependent—or to seize control of oil supplies on which much of western Europe depends. In either case both groups wonder if this invading force is coming to seize control of *their* economic assets.

But the ultimate target soon becomes clear. The target all along had been Israel.

ACTS OF GOD

Ezekiel predicts in advance how the invading force will be defeated. God Himself will act alone to defeat the invading army, demonstrating to Israel that He is God.

"'It will come about on that day, when Gog comes against the land of Israel,' declares the Lord GOD, 'that My fury will mount up in My anger. In My zeal and in My blazing wrath I declare that on that day there will surely be a great earthquake in the land of Israel'" (Ezekiel 38:18–19).

The ultimate "act of God"—a devastating earthquake at the precise time these invaders reach Israel—stops the armies in their tracks.

But God isn't finished.

In the confusion caused by the earthquake, "Every man's sword will be against his brother" (Ezekiel 38:21). In a major case of "friendly fire," the different groups will mistakenly begin attacking each other. The confusion caused by the earthquake is multiplied by the babble of languages.

God still isn't done.

"With pestilence and with blood I will enter into judgment with him; and I will rain on him and on his troops, and on the many peoples who are with him, a torrential rain, with hailstones, fire and brimstone" (Ezekiel 38:22).

A form of plague decimates the troops as hailstones and flooding rain pour down. And because of the earthquake,

"Every wall will fall to the ground." There will be no shelter where the invaders can hide. "Fire and brimstone" might describe the results of a volcanic eruption. The Golan Heights, which are the natural entry point for this northern army, are dotted with extinct volcanoes that could each, at the Lord's command, erupt in cataclismic fury.

God concludes: "I will magnify Myself, sanctify Myself, and make Myself known in the sight of many nations; and they will know that I am the Lord" (v. 23).

The effects of the battle will have international repercussions.

THE ULTIMATE CRISIS OF FAITH

With the destruction of this multinational army, the Islamic world will finally face a true crisis of faith. Their defeat will not have come at the hands of a superior military force. It will be God Himself who crushes the invaders. And this stunning defeat will shake their faith in everything they have believed. Once this happens they will be all the more receptive to the claims of a false Messiah who will announce that he is God incarnate.

In contrast, the Jewish people will come to the realization that their nation was just delivered from certain destruction by the hand of God. A national religious awakening will begin to take hold in Israel as the people turn back to their true God. Sometime later the leader from Europe returns to Israel and, according to the apostle Paul, "takes his seat in the temple of God, displaying himself as being God" (2 Thessalonians 2:4). But when he demands, "I'm God, worship me," Israel will say, "No, you're not." Why? Because they just witnessed the power of the true God at work.

ALL IN THE DETAILS

In addition to describing *who* will invade Israel and *what* will happen, Ezekiel also shares *when* it will happen. He first describes the time in general terms. "*After many days* you will be summoned; *in the latter years* you will come into the land that is restored from the sword, whose inhabitants have been gathered from many nations to the mountains of Israel which had been a continual waste" (Ezekiel 38:8, emphasis added). These nations will invade Israel sometime after the Jewish people return and resettle the land. From Ezekiel's perspective this invasion could have occurred any time after Israel was back in the land following its return from the Babylonian captivity in 539 BC. However, no such invasion ever took place from that time until the Jewish people were expelled again by the Romans. Nor has it taken place since the nation was reborn in 1948.

The prophecy remains unfulfilled.

According to Ezekiel, Israel must be back in the land, but they also must be living in relative safety. The people "have been gathered from many nations to the mountains of Israel . . . and they are living securely, all of them" (v. 8). Later God says to the invaders, "On that day when My people Israel are living securely, will you not know it?" (v. 14).

But Israel must also be experiencing genuine peace. As the invaders plot their attack, the leader says to himself, "I will go up against the land of unwalled villages. I will go against those who are at rest, that live securely, all of them living without walls and having no bars or gates" (v. 11).

Such walls, gates, and bars were protective measures common in Old Testament times to provide security against potential enemies. This predicted invasion will take place when

Israel finally feels genuinely secure and unthreatened. Those conditions certainly don't describe present-day Israel. Since 1948 Israel has never felt secure enough to lower her defenses. For over sixty-five years Israel hasn't been at peace. They've only experienced times when there has been an absence of war.

WHEN REAL PEACE COMES

When will Israel experience peace? The Bible identifies two such periods of time still to come. The first will occur for a very short period when a coming world leader "solves" the Middle East crisis by brokering an apparent peace between Israel and the Palestinians and other Arab neighbors. This period of relative peace will only last for three-and-a-half years, but during that time Israel will apparently feel secure.

The second period is ushered in when Jesus Christ returns to earth to set up His kingdom of peace. During His glorious reign on earth, the Bible declares that "He will judge between the nations, and will render decisions for many peoples; and they will hammer their swords into plowshares and their spears into pruning hooks. Nations will not lift up sword against nation, and never again will they learn war" (Isaiah 2:4).

So which time of peace is Ezekiel describing? While both periods of peace end with attacks against Israel, several specific statements in Ezekiel 38–39 point to the first period of peace as the one when the invasion will occur. The invasion serves as a wake-up call to Israel to rouse them from their spiritual lethargy and to turn them back to God. Since Israel is alive spiritually during the Messiah's thousand-year reign of peace (Isaiah 59:21; Jeremiah 31:31–34), the invasion described by Ezekiel must happen during the first time of peace when Israel is still spiritually insensitive.

Ezekiel provides a second clue as to when the invasion will happen. He says the invasion will take place when the nation of Israel is back in the land, but he also says it will take place *before* all the Jews have returned to the land. After describing the battle and its aftermath, God announces to His people, "Now I will restore the fortunes of Jacob and have mercy on the whole house of Israel; and I will be jealous for My holy name" (Ezekiel 39:25).

So one result of the invasion is the *final* restoration of the Jews to the land of Israel. Since all the Jewish people will return to the land at the time of Jesus' second coming (Matthew 24:31), this battle must take place before that final gathering at Christ's return.

So is this day near? We simply do not know. The next event on God's prophetic timetable is the removal of His church from earth. The prophetic clock does not begin ticking until that happens, and until the coming world leader signs an agreement with Israel. Sometime within the first three-and-a-half years after the signing of that agreement, the battle described by Ezekiel will occur. But world events do suggest the time may be approaching.

Russia is forging economic ties with Iran, and Turkey continues its drift away from the West and back toward its Islamic roots. Sudan and Libya lie in turmoil. The world is anxious to complete a comprehensive Middle East peace plan to resolve the Israeli–Palestinian crisis. And struggles over the supply and control of oil and natural gas resources are still behind much of the conflict in the Middle East. When world events mirror the events described in the Bible, the beginning of the end could be near.

All the while, ISIS continues its violent advance, capturing the attention of a horrified and watching world.

There must be a way to respond that matches the ultimate purposes and plans of God.

10

GOD'S BATTLE PLAN FOR VICTORY

These things I have spoken to you, so that in Me you may
have peace. In the world you have tribulation,
but take courage; I have overcome the world.

JESUS
John 16:33

The only thing we have to fear is fear itself—nameless, unreasoning, unjustified terror which paralyzes needed efforts to convert retreat into advance."[1] Those are the now timeless words of President Franklin D. Roosevelt, spoken during his first inaugural address to calm and to encourage a nation paralyzed by fear. The Great Depression had destroyed businesses and wiped out jobs, forcing families from their homes and farms. People who had worked all their lives now stood in long lines at soup kitchens waiting for a hot meal. For one of the few times in our nation's history, America feared the future.

Since September 11, 2001, the world has been battling another enemy—Islamic jihadists spreading across the world in a raging fire of violence. The war against radical Islamic terrorists is now in its second decade, and the threat is as real today as it was when the conflict began. The coalition against ISIS is just the latest struggle in what seems like a never-ending war. Is there a way to finally stop this threat?

Ultimately, worldwide peace will not come until the Prince of Peace returns to earth, according to the Scriptures. Two Old Testament prophets whose words offer great hope today, Isaiah and Micah, pointed to a time when humanity will finally "hammer their swords into plowshares and their spears into pruning hooks" (Isaiah 2:4; Micah 4:3). But until that day arrives, peace remains little more than an elusive dream. Does that mean we are doomed to live our lives in fear?

Thankfully, the answer is no. God has given His followers a battle plan to defeat the forces of darkness and evil.

First, we need to make clear an important distinction between what God expects from our government and what God expects from Christians. The apostle Paul reminded the church in Rome to "be in subjection to the governing authorities. For there is no authority except from God, and those which exist are established by God" (Romans 13:1). There are times when governments go beyond the boundaries set for them by God. And in those instances, we must choose whether we are to obey God or government. The actions of Daniel when told not to pray (Daniel 6) or Peter when told not to preach (Acts 5) are compelling reminders that "we must obey God rather than men" (Acts 5:29). Certainly believers living in the areas now controlled by ISIS must disobey when ordered to deny their faith.

God instituted human government, and its primary role is to protect its citizens and to promote peace. Our government has been doing that in its fight against Al-Qaeda and ISIS, and we need to support our leaders in those efforts. But we also need to realize that there are limits to what physical force can do. America has spent trillions of dollars, and lost thousands of lives, in its struggle to stop Al-Qaeda and ISIS, but the threat remains and has even intensified.

Is there another battle plan that could be more effective?

There is and it's God's battle plan for His followers. Here is His plan for victory over ISIS, and every other force for evil.

RECOGNIZE THE REAL ENEMY

We like to put faces to our fears. We want to see what our enemy looks like; to demystify him; to give him a tangibility that lets us stare him in the face so we can take him down. But sometimes that works against us.

When America made Saddam Hussein the ultimate enemy, we foolishly announced "Mission Accomplished" once he was captured. But the fight went on.

When we made "Osama bin Laden" world enemy number one, we declared that Al-Qaeda was "on the run" after his death. But the threat continued.

Could it be that all this time we've been pursuing the wrong enemy?

STILL OUR ANCIENT FOE

Martin Luther, the Protestant Reformer, penned his magnificent hymn "A Mighty Fortress Is Our God." In that hymn he brought keen insight to the nature of our true enemy, Satan. "For still our ancient foe, doth seek to work us woe; his craft and power are great, and armed with cruel hate; on earth is not his equal."[2]

Paul wrote his letter to the church in Ephesus while shackled to a soldier in Rome, under house arrest, and on trial for his life. His friends were concerned as they speculated on the different forces aligned against this outspoken apostle. Their list of possible suspects was long . . . and complex. Caesar, other Roman authorities, the Jewish religious leaders, even jealous Christians upset over Paul's popularity. But Paul pointed his readers in a different direction.

The real enemy facing Paul, and all other believers, wasn't to be found in Rome or Jerusalem. This enemy, and the battle he directs, extends into heaven itself. Paul declared that "our struggle is not against flesh and blood, but against . . . the spiritual forces of wickedness in the heavenly places" (Ephesians 6:12).

> For our struggle is not against flesh and blood, but against the rulers, against the powers, against the world forces of this darkness, against the spiritual forces of wickedness in the heavenly places.
>
> **The apostle Paul**
> **Ephesians 6:12**

The ultimate commander of ISIS remains unseen by most of his followers, but he is not unknown. This commander is Satan himself.

From the beginning Satan has opposed God and His righteous purposes. Satan tempted Adam and Eve to disobey God. Satan went into God's presence to accuse Job. Satan moves across the earth "like a roaring lion, seeking someone to devour" (1 Peter 5:8). Satan disguises himself as an angel of light to avoid detection (2 Corinthians 11:14).

He comes as the ultimate deceiver of the world (Revelation 12:9).

Many who are sucked in by Satan's deception believe they are actually serving God. Others listen to his lies and confuse rebellion with enlightenment.

ISIS isn't the real enemy. But driven by the real enemy's power, this group has the darkest and most evil intentions. Furthermore, ISIS represents a collection of lost individuals who have been deluded into believing a lie. Satan's power of delusion, coupled with humanity's own corrupt nature, makes *everyone* capable of committing the worst atrocities imaginable.

In fact the Bible teaches that all forces of evil are under Satan's command. But "greater is He who is in you than he who is in the world" (1 John 4:4).

Remarkably, the hope against this formidable foe is not to be found in military might or supersophisticated counterintelligence. The hope is the eternal Word of God. And in His Word God has revealed for us a three-pronged strategy for how Christians can face the real enemy at work in the world.

PUT ON YOUR ARMOR

After describing the spiritual battle facing the church in Ephesians 6, Paul ordered his readers to prepare for the conflict by putting on spiritual armor.

He writes, "Therefore, take up the full armor of God, so that you may be able to resist in the evil day, and having done everything, to stand firm" (Ephesians 6:13).

What sort of armor is appropriate for fighting a spiritual battle? The first item needed is *truth*. This can refer to the truth of God's Word, but in this passage it more likely refers to our own truthfulness. Satan is a crafty liar, and the best way to stand against him is to speak truthfully. "The truth, the whole truth, and nothing but the truth" is a good defense against Satan and all his ways.

The second piece of armor is *the breastplate of righteousness*. Since Paul is writing to those who have already placed their trust in God, the righteousness he has in mind is most likely not the righteousness received at salvation. Instead, he is referring to holy living. It's putting God's righteousness into practice in our daily lives—living out what we say we believe. If truth refers to *what we say*, righteousness refers to *how we act*. Satan is a master of deception and duplicity, so the best way to defend ourselves is by living a life of integrity and holiness.

The third piece of armor is having our feet shod with the *preparation of the gospel of peace*. This is a bit confusing at first. Sharing the good news about Jesus is one way to understand what Paul is saying, but it doesn't seem to fit with the idea that these early pieces of armor are a defense against Satan's attacks. Perhaps Paul has in mind that we need to make sure we are standing firmly on the reality that the good news about Jesus is what will ultimately bring peace. Knowing that God's message of forgiveness through Jesus Christ can penetrate the hardest of hearts allows us to stand firm in our faith while not getting drawn into Satan's destructive tactics.

The *shield of faith* is the next defensive piece of armor, and it's specifically designed to "extinguish all the flaming arrows of the evil one." One of Satan's greatest tactics is to get us to doubt God's greatness and love by placing negative thoughts into our minds. From his first encounter with Eve in Genesis 3:1 ("Did God actually say . . . ?"), Satan has tried to steal our confidence in God by planting seeds of doubt. The "faith" here isn't God's faith in us; it's our faith in Him. It's being able to cry out when we don't understand what God seems to be doing, "Though He slay me, I will hope in Him" (Job 13:15). It is constantly reminding ourselves that "life is tough, but God is good . . . all the time!"

The last pieces of armor a soldier would grab before heading into battle were his *helmet* and his *sword* (Ephesians 6:17). And both are also essential in this spiritual battle.

The *helmet of salvation* is our clear understanding that God has rescued us from sin and will continue to deliver us from Satan's attacks. It's remembering that Jesus will do for us what He did for Simon Peter the night of His betrayal. "Simon, Simon, behold, Satan has demanded permission to sift you like wheat; but I have prayed for you, that your faith may not fail" (Luke 22:31–32).

The *sword* is the only offensive weapon given to us to fight against Satan. And Paul describes it as "the sword of the Spirit, which is the word of God." The very weapon Jesus used to fight off Satan's temptation in the wilderness is the same one God wants us to have by our side. Never underestimate the power of God's Word!

Paul ends his weapons-training session by describing the way in which the soldier is to use these weapons in combat. The best-equipped soldier still must remain in constant contact with his commanding officer and be ever vigilant. Paul tells his readers to "pray at all times" and to "be on the alert with all perseverance" (Ephesians 6:18). The enemy will attack in unexpected ways and at unexpected times. So the best way for us to stay prepared is not by standing in our own defense but by kneeling in prayer and seeking wisdom, strength, and power from the God who fights on our behalf.

DEMONSTRATE THE RIGHT ATTITUDE

Wearing the right armor is important, but so is going into battle with the right attitude. Jesus shared this part of God's strategic plan in Luke 6:27–28. "But I say to you who hear, love your enemies, do good to those who hate you, bless those who curse you, pray for those who mistreat you."

This strategic attitude is counterintuitive, which is what makes it so effective.

The Bible's truth of God's unconditional love for humanity is a truth not found in the Quran. Love is not one of the ninety-nine names for God found there. The god of Islam can love people for what they do, but it's only a performance-based love. The idea of love existing as part of the very essence of God doesn't exist in Islam. And that's what makes Jesus' words so revolutionary.

Daniel Miller, who oversees the training of Arab world leaders for ministry with the mission organization Pioneers, conducted a survey of several hundred Saudi Arabian students studying in the United States.[3] One question he asked was "What is your view of Americans in general?" The response was compelling. An overwhelming majority of the responders answered that Americans were extremely friendly, but they were lousy at *being friends*. In other words, Americans are nice, but too busy and distracted serving themselves to have any margin left for building authentic and loving relationships with people different from themselves.

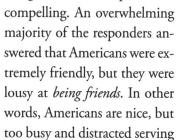

Allah of the Koran is not a God of love. He is so transcendent that he cannot love people.

Wade Akins
Sharing Your Faith with Muslims[4]

One of the most powerful things Christians can do to prevent groups like ISIS from making inroads is to demonstrate the love of Jesus to every Muslim they meet. They can stop and say a kind word to Muslim neighbors and coworkers. Befriending a Muslim might mean inviting him or her out for coffee. Before your time together, pray for them. Ask God to open the door so you can share the reason for your love—which is the love of Christ.

Satan has no effective countermeasure to someone demonstrating the love and goodness of Christ.

STAND FIRM IN YOUR FAITH

In Revelation 12 the apostle John describes a still-future battle that will unfold in heaven. Though not seen from earth, this battle will impact the course of human history. In this cosmic conflict, Satan and his followers will once and for all be purged from heaven and confined to the earth. Satan will respond to his banishment by doing everything possible to destroy this planet we call home. "Woe to the earth and the sea, because the devil has come down to you, having great wrath, knowing that he has only a short time" (Revelation 12:12).

In describing this coming scene of chaos, John pauses to describe how those on earth will overcome Satan even during the most hellish time the world will ever know. And their secret is also one we can use today to defeat Satan and any forces under his command. John shares this secret in three staccato phrases, recorded in verse 11: "And they overcame him because of the blood of the Lamb and because of the word of their testimony, and they did not love

> We think we are in the land of the living on our way to the land of the dying. Nothing could be further from the biblical truth. You and I are in the land of the dying on our way to the land of the living.
> **Professor Howard G. Hendricks**[5]

their life even when faced with death" (Revelation 12:11).

Each ensuing phrase is significant. These believers overcame . . .

- *Because of the blood of the Lamb.* The ultimate move to defeat Satan took place two thousand years ago in Jerusalem. When Jesus died on the cross, He paid the penalty for humanity's sin by shedding His own blood. Three days later He demonstrated His power over death. Battles against Satan and his forces are still taking place, but the ultimate victory has already been secured. The outcome is *not* in doubt.

- *Because of the word of their testimony.* Satan is the master deceiver, but God's faithful followers can counter his influence by sharing God's truthful message. As John Walvoord once noted, "The word of the believer's testimony opposes the deceiving work of Satan in that the preaching of the gospel is the power of God unto salvation."[5]

- *Because they did not love their life even when faced with death.* The greatest weapon Satan uses to intimidate humanity is fear—especially fear of death. But this weapon is only effective against followers of Jesus if we allow it to be, because Jesus has already defeated death. Once we realize that physical death isn't the end of our existence, we are freed from that paralyzing fear.

God has a plan for defeating the forces of spiritual darkness. That plan is also effective against ISIS and any other alliance used by Satan to try to force darkness and chaos on the world. But what difference does any of this make in your life today? That's perhaps the most important question still remaining to be answered.

STAYING CALM IN CHAOS

Be careful whom you choose to hate. The small and the vulnerable own a
protection great enough, if you could but see it, to melt you into jelly.
Beware those who reside beneath the shadow of the Wings.

LEIF ENGER
Peace Like a River[1]

Not too long ago my family and I (Mark) were in a local
restaurant enjoying an evening meal. The restaurant sits
nestled in the small college town where we live—a community in which students from around the world have come to
pursue an American education. On that particular night, two
Arab students were at an adjacent table enjoying a lively conversation in Arabic. Above our heads a flat screen television
streamed the latest CNN coverage of intensifying ISIS violence in Syria.

I found myself becoming increasingly uncomfortable as the
two students' conversation grew more animated. Others in
the restaurant looked visibly uncomfortable too. Customers
began to fidget. One family, clearly anxious, paid their bill
and promptly left the restaurant.

Somehow, those two students represented all the angst and uneasiness I had been feeling about the ISIS situation half the world away. When they should have otherwise been seen as part of the multicultural fabric of a typical university town, these young Saudi students had unknowingly become objects of suspicion and reproach, and victims of my own prejudice and fear.

The connection was sadly obvious.

My anxious mind imagined the worst. These Arab students, seemingly minding their own business and enjoying an evening meal, could actually be members of an ISIS sleeper cell plotting a terror attack right here in our quiet Midwestern town! And at that moment I felt shame and regret and realized fear had hijacked my senses.

To be honest, it was that situation that compelled me to talk with Charles Dyer—my good friend and colleague "Charlie"—about collaborating on this book. My sentiments, though easily understandable, don't seem to mesh with what Christians truly believe. And I am a pastor!

It is so easy to respond in fear and operate out of a reactionary mentality. But we know there's a better way. That night in the restaurant, what I needed was both understanding and perspective. I was operating from a deficit in both regards.

QUESTIONS OF JUSTICE ... AND VENGEANCE

Yet, somehow we justify our prejudice by pointing to the horrifying tactics of ISIS. *How many more gruesome murders and torturous advances are these monsters going to be allowed to commit before we really get serious and remove them from the face of the earth? Why are we just seemingly sitting here and not unleashing the maximum force of American technology and military might to wipe out this growing threat? Why do they want to live here, right next to us, anyway? Don't they know they don't fit in here?*

I know we've all felt those feelings and somehow they seem justified in our minds. But is that really the heart of God for us? Does He want us to hunker down in fear and anger and seek revenge against ISIS and all who are associated with them? Or has He called us to a more compassionate and self-less response? And if so, how is such a response even possible?

AN OTHERWORLDLY PERSPECTIVE

Two generations ago five young men left the comforts and promise of America to journey to the jungles of Ecuador. Their goal was to bring the gospel of Christ to the Auca Indians, a primitive, unreached tribe renowned for their violent and murderous ways. The Aucas (now called the Waorani) had been responsible for the ruthless murders of several Shell Oil Company associates who had ventured into their territory in hopes of finding oil.

Yet Jim Elliot, missionary pilot Nate Saint, and the other three men were committed to reaching these people with the love and compassion of Christ. They set out in spite of all conventional wisdom at the time, determined to bring the gospel to the Aucas. After much preparation, including the dropping of gifts from the air to show their good intentions, contact was finally made, meeting on the ground with a couple of the natives. Several days later the five missionaries spotted ten Aucas from the air, and radioed the base they were landing on a sandbar deep in the jungle. Support missionaries at the base awaited word of the encounter.

But the report didn't come. Only static and silence. Days went by, and still more silence.

Eventually a search party was dispatched to discover the whereabouts of the five men. It wasn't long before it was clear that what was feared most had become reality. All five were dead. Their bodies lay strewn across the sand, broken and marred from the lethal blows of spears and machetes. The news of their violent deaths sent shockwaves across the world. Christians sat in horror and disbelief. Many called for revenge in response to this senseless act.

Shortly before the young men left for Ecuador, Jim Elliot's wife, Elisabeth, asked her husband if he and the other four missionaries would defend themselves with guns if they were attacked by the Aucas. Jim responded, "We will not use our guns. Because we are ready for heaven, but they are not."[2]

Such a response can only be explained one way. Jim Elliot was willing to face danger—even to the point of laying down his life for the gospel—because he chose to live every day by faith, not fear. He knew his life was safely sheltered "in the shadow of the Almighty" (Psalm 91:1). He knew his eternal destiny was sure. And he knew God was in control.

In the face of such mounting uncertainty in the Middle East, and in our own fractured worlds, we as Christians can rise above the fray and shine as bright lights against the darkness of ISIS. Like Jim Elliot and his fellow missionaries, all of us can reflect a calm amid the chaos when we have the presence of Christ within our lives.

FAITH NOT FEAR: THERE IS A BETTER WAY

We know how unsettling the ISIS crisis makes us feel. And in so many ways, our fears may seem justified. But the Bible makes plain that God has provided to those who trust in Him " not . . . a spirit of fear, but of power and of love and of a sound mind" (2 Timothy 1:7 NKJV). Our response to ISIS, and any other outward threat, needs to come from God, not from ourselves.

We must respond as Jesus would respond, regardless of what's at stake . . .

At times, life can be excruciatingly difficult. Few of us can imagine the torturous plight of the men, women, and children suffering under these ISIS extremists. The horrors boggle the mind. Yet none of us is exempt from having to fight life's hardest battles. Cancer, divorce, financial hardships, tragic accidents, and the unexpected deaths of family and friends are just a few of the many all-too-common experiences that roil all our lives.

So what gives? Even for Christians—men and women sincerely trying to do what's right—there are times when life seems to go horribly wrong. And the question we often ask ourselves at such times is *Where is God?* Where is His mighty power when the barometer drops to bottom of the gauge? What is His purpose in applying such negative pressure to His most faithful followers? Thankfully, the Word of God provides both comfort and perspective.

An ancient hymn, from the heart of David, helps point the way forward. Consider his words from Psalm 11:

In the LORD I take refuge; . . .
How can you say to my soul, "Flee as a bird to your mountain;
For, behold, the wicked bend the bow,
They make ready their arrow upon the string to shoot in darkness at the upright in heart.

If the foundations are destroyed, what can the righteous
   do?"
The LORD is in His holy temple; the LORD's throne is in
   heaven;
His eyes behold, His eyelids test the sons of men.
The LORD tests the righteous and the wicked,
And the one who loves violence His soul hates.
Upon the wicked He will rain snares;
Fire and brimstone and burning wind will be the por-
   tion of their cup.
For the LORD is righteous, He loves righteousness;
The upright will behold His face.

In Psalm 11, David, the shepherd king of Israel and a man after God's own heart (Acts 13:22), is facing the battle of his life. For David, it felt very much like the world was coming unhinged. As he watched the wicked run roughshod over the righteous, he must have experienced the same emotions we feel as we watch image after image of ISIS's barbaric assault on the innocent.

So what do we do when we feel like the foundation is crumbling? What should be our perspective? What can we know and learn about God, no matter what the outcome? There are really only two possible responses—the response of fear or the response of faith.

THE RESPONSE OF FEAR—FLEEING AND FRETTING

The crisis that David faced was no minor headache. This was not David with the sniffles, a torn ligament, or trying to manage his soldiers with dwindling supplies. This was David on the brink—clearly facing the battle of his life as his enemies closed in. And in this prayer of anguished appeal, we see the desperate insufficiency of the human experience set against the wondrous, powerful purposes of a sovereign and all-seeing God.

In your response to ISIS, or any other unsettling circumstances you face, fear can tempt you to respond in two very unhealthy ways.

First, *you are tempted to take matters into your own hands.*

In the midst of his trial, David had numerous advisers telling him what to do. "How can you say to my soul, 'Flee as a bird to your mountain . . . ?'" That seems just like the human response, doesn't it? It's similar to the empty, ill-timed advice Job's friends gave after their suffering friend lost his health, his herds, and far worse, all his children. At times such thoughts come from our own inner voice, too, telling us the same thing. *It's as bad as could be imagined.*

One natural response to fear can be flight. Run away! Flee! Somebody had David's ear and was telling him, quite literally, to run for the hills. "David, it's over! Take matters into your own hands or you're not going to make it." Too many Christians respond in the same way to situations like ISIS, the Ebola outbreak, an economy in a tailspin, or any other trial that feels completely out of control. When the ground begins to move under our feet, fear tempts us to cut and run.

Second, *fear tempts you to focus on circumstances rather than on God.*

David describes in compelling detail how "the wicked bend the bow," and "make ready their arrow upon the string to shoot in darkness" (11:2). Fear can cause us to become hyperfocused on the what-ifs of our situation, regardless of whether such things actually ever occur.

David's fear that the very foundations of his kingdom were about to crumble (v. 3) suggests he was being tempted to expect the very worst possible outcome. We can easily do the same. But such exaggerated thoughts and patterns of worry are incongruous with what we know to be absolutely true. Remember, God is in control, and our confidence needs to remain in Him.

THE RESPONSE OF FAITH—TRUSTING AND REJOICING

Somewhere in the white space between the end of verse 3 and the beginning of verse 4, David regains his spiritual footing . . . and his faith.

David declares, "The LORD is in His holy temple; the LORD's throne is in heaven." His confidence transitions from relying on himself, or his own resources, to trusting in the power and sovereign purposes of the Lord.

Regardless of the difficulty and severity of our situation, we, like David, can turn to God. He is the only one who can heal, deliver, transform, calm the storm, and make a new creation. Only He can change the situation.

The direction of David's faith swings dramatically from focusing on his circumstances here on earth, to placing his confidence in the God of heaven. "The LORD is in His holy temple." When David declares that the Lord is on His throne, he demonstrates his confidence that the Lord is in control. God does not lose sight of us when life begins to unravel. And the Lord sees everything from the vantage point of heaven— whether it be the problems David was facing, or the evil of ISIS today.

Remember, the Lord knows all the details of our circumstances. He knows the cause and He knows the outcome. He sees all, knows all, and controls all.

When we turn to God in the face of difficulty, our perspective changes completely. We now see Him, exalted over everything else. Fear magnifies circumstances. Faith magnifies the Lord. What is topmost in your mind or heart? Is it your financial difficulties? Your broken marriage? Your addiction? Your past failures? Is it your children? Your uncertain future? Like David, you need to turn to the Lord and allow Him to change your perspective.

David's new confidence not only focuses on the sovereign control of God but also on His perfect justice. "The Lord tests the righteous, and the wicked, and the one who loves violence His soul hates" (v. 5). God is the only perfect, righteous Judge of all the earth. He knows everyone's motives and actions, and He will ultimately give each person what he or she deserves. This includes ultimate justice for members of ISIS. The wicked, the ruthless, and those who love violence will face a certain and dreadful judgment.

"The Lord tests the righteous and the wicked, and the one who loves violence His soul hates. Upon the wicked He will rain snares; fire and brimstone and burning wind will be the portion of their cup" (vv. 5–6). David is convinced that God will ultimately deal with everyone fairly and justly. He knows the wicked will eventually pay a heavy price for their deeds. God does allow trials to come into the lives of the righteous to test them and to strengthen their faith in Him. But His judgment on those who are evil will be comprehensive and severe.

That is a surety of eternity.

DURING OUR STORMS OF FEAR

Finally, David's resolve in trouble is to trust in the Lord's totally reliable and often unexpected personal and powerful presence: "The upright will behold His face" (v. 7).

This is God showing up in the middle of the storm. The Hebrew idiom speaks to God personally coming to the aid of the righteous in their time of trouble. No matter how horrifying the trial, the Lord promises His personal and powerful presence to the one who trusts in Him. Picture God saying to each of us: "In those times when you feel most alone, terribly abandoned, and desperately in need, I will personally come to your side. You can count on it."

When my son Jacob was little, his mother and I made a big deal when he transitioned from his crib into his *big boy bed*. But Jacob was afraid of the dark. At bedtime, he often wanted me to lie beside him and sing. Most nights I'd sing a hymn or two as he calmed his little mind and drifted off to sleep. As I sang, he'd slowly relax. Every few seconds his little body would twitch, then relax, twitch, then relax. At the end of every hymn, Jacob would reach back behind him and put his hand on my shoulder, making certain I had not left the room.

I kept singing.

Reassured, he'd roll back over and close his eyes. A few more minutes would pass in the darkness and quietness, and he would reach back again. As I felt his little hand on my shoulder, I would assure him again I wasn't going to leave.

I kept singing. Over and over, he'd turn and I'd let him hear my voice.

This little ritual continued until he eventually drifted off to sleep. Afraid of the dark, he needed assurance that his father was still by his side. (One of those hymns concludes this chapter.)

GOD'S PROMISE OF HIS PRESENCE

Perhaps you need that assurance too. God has promised to never leave you or forsake you (Deuteronomy 31:6).[3] He has loved you with an everlasting love. He sent His Son, Jesus Christ, to die for your sin, to pay the penalty of death, and to shed His blood. By putting your faith in Jesus, you become a child of God—and in becoming His child, you receive all the promises of the heavenly Father, including the promise of Psalm 11. You will see His face. You will live in eternity with Him.

Until that day, you don't have to live your life in fear. He is in absolute control of everything in your life. And in those times when you feel most afraid, uncertain, and doubting your ability to get through one more day, all you have to do is turn to Him. He has personally promised to come to your side and provide the comfort you need.

It's possible you picked up this book because you had a strong interest in the ISIS crisis. We hope you have a clearer understanding of the situation and players involved and have gained, as a result, a calmer and more compassionate perspective.

But maybe you've realized, too, that you're living your life hiding in the shadows of fear. Because of your circumstances, perhaps you feel like David, that all hope is lost.

If that's the case, we urge you to turn to the Lord. Reach through the dark for Him and put your trust in Him. You will hear His voice; you will find His personal and powerful presence. He says to you in your darkness, *I'm here. I'm here. I'm here. I'm here. I'm not going to leave you. I'm here. I'm here.*

JACOB'S BEDTIME HYMN

"How Firm a Foundation"

Fear not, I am with thee; O be not dismayed,
For I am thy God, I will still give thee aid;
I'll strengthen thee, help thee, and cause thee to stand,
Upheld by My gracious, omnipotent hand.

When through fiery trials thy pathway shall lie,
My grace, all sufficient, shall be thy supply;
The flame shall not hurt thee; I only design
Thy dross to consume and thy gold to refine.

The soul that on Jesus hath leaned for repose,
I will not, I will not desert to its foes;
That soul, though all hell should endeavor to shake,
I'll never, no, never, no, never forsake![4]

ACKNOWLEDGMENTS

The authors wish to give a special word of gratitude to the many people who have helped make *The ISIS Crisis* a reality. First, we are grateful to Greg Thornton, senior vice president of media, and Paul Santhouse, vice president and publisher, both at Moody Global Ministries, for their enthusiasm and vision for the book. We also wish to thank Randall Payleitner, editorial director at Moody Publishers, for his steady hand of guidance every step of the way. Also, thank you, Jim Vincent, for your careful eye and genuine concern for the well-being of the manuscript as we kept your in-box full over a period of several weeks. And thank you, Janis Backing, for keeping the vision alive and for your gracious sorting through of all our wild and crazy publicity ideas, as you helped guide the book to readers.

We also are grateful for the help of our wives. Thank you, Kathy Dyer, for your sharp watch over the project, proofreading the manuscript in batches before sending it off to Moody Publishers. And thank you, Tracy Tobey, for your abiding patience and unfailing understanding as we moved forward with another project during a busy holiday season.

Finally, we extend a heartfelt expression of gratitude to the countless American servicemen and women standing courageously on the front lines for freedom's cause in some of the darkest and most dangerous places of the world. You are among the many of whom this world is not worthy. We are grateful to you and your families for the sacrifices you make every day.

To God be the glory.

NOTES

Introduction: ISIS on the Move

1. When discussing the jihadists in Iraq, President Obama said, "The analogy we use around here sometimes, and I think is accurate, is that if a jayvee team puts on Lakers uniforms that doesn't make them Kobe Bryant." David Remnick, "Going the Distance: On and Off the Road with Barack Obama," *New Yorker*, January 27, 2014.
2. See Lizzie Dearden, "Isis vs Islamic State vs Isil vs Daesh: What Do the Different Names Mean—and Why Does It Matter?", *The Independent*, September 23, 2014, http://www.independent.co.uk/news/world/middle-east/isis-vs-islamic-state-vs-isil-vs-daesh-what-do-the-different-names-mean-9750629.html, cf. Jaime Fuller, "'ISIS' vs. 'ISIL' vs. 'Islamic State': The Political Importance of a Much Debated Acronym," *Washington Post*, September 9, 2014, http://www.washingtonpost.com/blogs/the-fix/wp/2014/09/09/isis-vs-isil-vs-islamic-state-the-political-importance-of-a-much-debated-acronym.

Chapter 1: The War to End War

1. George Santanya, *Life of Reason*, vol. 1: *Reason in Common Sense* (New York: Scribner's, 1905), 284.
2. ISIL is another name for ISIS. See note 2 in the introduction.
3. The phrase came from a book written by H. G. Wells, *The War That Will End War* (New York: Duffield & Company, 1914) in which he argued that the defeat of Prussian imperialism could bring about an end to all war.
4. For an excellent study of all the issues, read David Fromkin, *A Peace to End All Peace: The Fall of the Ottoman Empire and the Creation of the Modern Middle East* (New York: Avon Books, 1989).
5. Letter from Henry McMahon to Hussein dated October 24, 1915.
6. Letter from Arthur James Balfour to Baron Rothschild dated November 2, 1917.
7. Richard Engel, *NBC Nightly News*, June 28, 2014.

Chapter 2: The Rise of the Mujahideen

1. Jimmy Carter, address to the nation following the Soviet invasion of Afghanistan, January 4, 1980. Online by Gerhard Peters and John T. Woolley, *The American Presidency Project*, http://www.presidency.ucsb.edu/ws/?pid=32911.
2. "Sadat Assassinated at Army Parade as Men amid Ranks Fire into Stands; Vice President Affirms 'All Treaties,'" *New York Times,* October 6, 1981.

3. Ruhollah Khomeini, remarks to students and educators in Qom, Iran, March 13, 1979.
4. Attributed to Saddam Hussein by Latif Yahia, double for Uday Hussein. "I Knew Saddam," Al Jazeera English radio broadcast, July 31, 2007.
5. President Carter's Address to the Nation on the Soviet Invasion of Afghanistan, January 4, 1980.
6. Quote from Congressman Charlie Wilson in "Charlie Did It," *60 Minutes*, CBS-TV, October 30, 1988, produced by George Crile.

Chapter 3: Connecting the Dots

1. Donald Rumsfeld, interview with Steve Croft, Infinity CBS Radio, November 14, 2002.
2. Steve Jobs, Stanford University Commencement address, June 12, 2005.
3. Thomas Joscelyn, "Al-Qaeda renews its oath of allegiance to Taliban leader Mullah Omar," *The Long War Journal*, July 21, 2014.
4. Mullah Omar in his own words, *The Guardian*, September 26, 2001.
5. Surah 48:10. "Behold, all who pledge their allegiance to thee pledge their allegiance to God: the hand of God is over their hands. Hence, he who breaks his oath, breaks it only to his own hurt; whereas he who remains true to what he has pledged unto God, on him will He bestow a reward supreme."
6. Text of *fatwa* urging jihad against Americans, published in *Al-Quds Al-Arabi*, February 23, 1998.
7. Ben Hubbard, "The Franchising of Al-Qaeda," *New York Times*, January 25, 2014.
8. Joseph Biden, remarks during a White House briefing, April 19, 2010.
9. ISIS is an acronym for the Islamic State of Iraq and Syria or the Islamic State of Iraq and al-Sham ("al-Sham" referring to the former Byzantine territories of "the east," which included greater Syria). ISIL is an acronym for the Islamic State of Iraq and the Levant.
10. Letter from Al-Qaeda chief Ayman al-Zawahiri, 2013.
11. "Jewish Museum Gun Suspect 'Was Captor in Syria,'" BBC News Europe, September 6, 2014, http://www.bbc.com/news/world-europe-29095044.

Chapter 4: The Rule of Hate

1. As cited in Benny Morris, *1948: A History of the First Arab-Israeli War* (New Haven, Mass.: Yale Univ. Press, 2009), 393.
2. Ibid.
3. Quote from a sermon by Ayatollah Khamenei, December 15, 2000.
4. "Anti-Jewish Violence in Pre-State Palestine/1929 Massacres," Committee for Accuracy in Middle East Reporting in America, August 23, 2009.
5. David Wollenberg, "The Myth of Jewish 'Colonialism': Demographics and Development in Palestine," *Harvard Israel Review*, 2003.
6. *Great Britain and Palestine*, 1915–1945, Information Paper no. 20, 3d ed. (London: Royal Institute for International Affairs, 1946), 64.

7. Morris, *1948*, 420.

8. Haj Amin al-Husseini, Grand Mufti of Jerusalem, Radio broadcast from Berlin, March 1, 1944.

9. "Muhammad," in Mitchell G. Bard, *The Complete Idiot's Guide to the Middle East Conflict*, 3d. ed. (New York: Penguin/Alpha, 2005), 51.

10. John Kerry, remarks at Third Annual Transformational Trends Policy Forum, November 17, 2014.

Chapter 5: A Kingdom Divided against Itself: Sunnis vs. Shiites

1. Sun Tzu, *The Art of War*, 3.18.

2. US Department of Education, Institute of Education Sciences, National Center for Education Statistics, National Assessment of Educational Progress (NAEP), 1994, 2001, and 2010 Geography Assessments.

3. Kyle Dropp, Joshua D. Kertzer, and Thomas Zeitzoff, "The Less Americans Know about Ukraine's Location, the More They Want U.S. to Intervene," *Washington Post*, April 7, 2014.

4. "The Sunni-Shia Divide," The Council on Foreign Relations, 2014. www.cfr.org/peace-conflict-and-human-rights/sunni-shia-divide/p33176#!/

5. Sun Tzu, *The Art of War*. 3.18.

Chapter 6: Variations on a Theme: The Composition of Islam

1. "Remarks by the President on Egypt," Office of the Press Secretary, February 11, 2011.

2. "The Arizona Republican Presidential Debate," February 22, 2012.

3. "Statement by President Barak Obama on ISIL," the White House, September 10, 2014.

4. Ibid.

5. *The History of Al-Tabari*, Vol. 8: *The Victory of Islam*, trans. Michael Fishbein (Albany: State Univ. of New York Press, 1997), 35.

6. "Sunnis and Shias: Islam's ancient schism," BBC News Middle East, June 20, 2014.

7. Bernard Lewis, "Islam and Liberal Democracy: A Historical Overview," *Journal of Democracy* 7, no. 2 (1996): 52–63. Copyright © 1996 National Endowment for Democracy and the Johns Hopkins University Press; https://www.mtholyoke.edu /acad/intrel/blewis.htm.

8. "EU warns Turkish army over vote," BBC News, April 28, 2007.

9. Orhan Oguz Gürbüz, "Is Turkey moving away from the democratic Western bloc?", *Today's Zaman*, March 15, 2014.

10. "US' Bass admits Turkey drifting towards authoritarianism," *Today's Zaman*, July 16, 2014.

11. Darrell Williams, "Western Democracy vs. Islamic Democracy: Iraq Politics," *Islam Daily*, May 9, 2008.

12. Article 4 [Islamic Principle] of the Iranian Government Constitution, 1979.

13. These quotations are from an unclassified US Defense Intelligence Agency translation of "Al-Qaida Constitutional Charter, Rules and Regulations," August 11, 2002.

14. Aaron Y Zelin, "Abu Bakr al-Baghdadi: Islamic State's driving force," BBC News Middle East, July 30, 2014.

15. Ayatollah Khomeini, "The Form of Islamic Governance," Al-Islam.org. The beginning of understanding is to appreciate that resolving this situation is immensely complex.

Chapter 7: Oil and Water: Seeing the Big Picture

1. Tony Blair, "Iraq, Syria and the Middle East—An essay," Office of Tony Blair, June 14, 2014.

2. David Fromkin, *A Peace to End All Peace: The Fall of the Ottoman Empire and the Creation of the Modern Middle East* (New York: Avon Books, 1989), 224.

3. A. Heidborn, *Manuel de Droit Public et Administratif de L'Empire Ottoman*, vol. 1 (Vienne: C. W. Stern, 1908), 8.

4. For example, Mark Twain described a road in Syria being "filled with . . . long processions of camels," which, when standing, looked like "an ostrich with an extra set of legs." Mark Twain, *The Innocents Abroad* (Hartford, Conn.: American Publishing 1869), 489.

5. Karl Baedeker, *Palestine and Syria*, 5th ed. (Leipzig: Karl Baedeker, 1912), 113.

6. The night he was assassinated, President Lincoln supposedly told his wife he wanted to visit Jerusalem (Stephen Mansfield, *Lincoln's Battle with God* [Nashville: Thomas Nelson, 2012]).

7. Fromkin, *A Peace to End All Peace*, 558.

8. Lee Smith, "Iraqi Insurgents Boast They're Building an Arab Super-State," Hudson Institute, June 12, 2014.

9. Amitzia Baram, quoted in C. S. Manegold and R. Wilkinson, "The Anchor and the Hope of the Weak and the Meek," *Newsweek*, August 13, 1990, 23.

10. Dalit Halevy and Ari Yashar, "Arab MK Calls for Establishment of 'United Islamic States,'" *Arutz Sheva*, October 3, 2014.

11. Bernard Lewis, "Iran in History," paper presented at the Mortimer and Raymond Sackler Institute of Advanced Studies at Tel Aviv University, January 18, 1999, 1.

12. Latif Nsayyif Jassim, Iraqi Minister of Information and Culture, *Baghdad Observer*, September 23, 1987, 2.

13. Marwan Bishara, "Why Arabs Fear a U.S.–Iran Détente," *New York Times*, October 27, 2013.

14. Yaakov Lappin, "Saudi Missile Parade a Signal to Iran, Israeli Defense Expert Tells 'Post,'" May 1, 2014.

15. "Water-Shortage Crisis Escalating in the Tigris–Euphrates Basin," Future Directions International, August 28, 2012.

16. John Vidal, "Water Supply Key to Outcome of Conflicts in Iraq and Syria, Experts Warn," *The Guardian*, July 2, 2014.

17. Suleiman al-Khalidi, "Middle East Drought a Threat to Global Food Prices," *Reuters*, May 7, 2014.

18. Tom Doyle, *Desperation* (Plano, TX: e3 Partners, 2011), 116.

19. "It was a 'mistake' not to take the fight to ISIS says ex-Kurdistan PM," *Rudaw*, February 10, 2014.

Chapter 8: Will ISIS Lead to Armageddon?

1. "Islamic State leader Baghdadi urges attacks in Saudi Arabia," *Irish Times*, November 14, 2014.

2. In addition to jihadist groups in Algeria, Egypt, and Libya that have pledged their support to ISIS, other jihadists offering support are in Chechnya (Thomas Joscelyn, "Chechen-led group swears allegiance to head of Islamic State of Iraq and Sham," *The Long War Journal* [November 27, 2013]); Gaza (Asmaa al-Ghoul, "Gaza Salafists Pledge Allegiance to ISIS," *AL-Monitor*, February 27, 2014); Lebanon ("Lebanese Group Pledges Allegiance to ISIS and the 'Islamic Caliphate,'" *Middle East Monitor*, July 1, 2014); Nigeria ("Boko Haram voices support for ISIS' Baghdadi," *Al Arabiya News*, July 13, 2014); Pakistan ("Pakistan: Tehrik-i-Taliban Pakistan Declares Allegiance to Islamic State," *Stratfor Global Intelligence*, Saturday, October 4, 2014); the Philippines ("Philippine Militants Pledge Allegiance to ISIS," *The Daily Star*, August 15, 2014); and Uzbekistan ("Uzbekistan: Islamist Leader Announces Alignment with Islamic State Militants," *Stratfor Global Intelligence*, Saturday, October 6, 2014).

3. For example, see *Daily Mail Online*: Jack Crone, "Wanted—experienced oil plant manager, pay £140,000 p.a. . . . send CV to ISIS: Jihadists advertising for skilled professionals to man its failing oil fields after string of fatal accidents," *Daily Mail Online*, November 19, 2014.

4. Jamie Weinstein, "ISIS Threatens America: 'We Will Raise the Flag of Allah in the White House,'" *The Daily Caller*, August 8, 2014.

5. Joel Richardson, *The Islamic Antichrist* (Los Angeles: WND Books, 2009), 171–75.

6. Ibid, 69.

7. For additional information on Daniel 9, see John F. Walvoord, *Daniel*, rev. and ed. by Charles H. Dyer and Philip E. Rawley (Chicago: Moody, 2012), 270–71.

Chapter 9: ISIS Eclipsed: The Ultimate Islamic Threat

1. John Kerry, "Remarks at a Reception in Honor of Eid al-Adha," October 16, 2014.

2. Leslie C. Allen, *Ezekiel 20–48*, Word Biblical Commentary (Dallas: Word, 1998), 204–5.

3. Lamar Eugene Cooper, *Ezekiel*, The New American Commentary (Nashville: Broadman & Holman, 1994), 332.

4. The NASB translates the Hebrew word *rosh* as a proper noun—"prince of Rosh." The question is whether Rosh should be translated as a proper

noun, identifying it as a place, or as an adjective. As noted in *The Bible Knowledge Commentary*, "'Rosh' never appears as a nation in any other biblical list of place names while all the other names are well attested (cf. Gen. 10:1–7; 1 Chron. 1:5–7; Ezek. 27:13–24; 32:26). One possible exception might be Isaiah 66:19 (NASB) but this is doubtful (see NIV)"; in Charles H. Dyer, "Ezekiel," *The Bible Knowledge Commentary*, ed. J. F. Walvoord and R. B. Zuck (Wheaton: Victor Books, 1985), 1,299.

5. Cooper, *Ezekiel*, 331.

6. The historian Josephus identified Togarmah with the Phrygians (Josephus Antiquities 1.6.1).

7. In the sixteenth century Elijah Levita produced *Tishbi*, a dictionary of 712 words used in the Talmud and Midrash, with their Yiddish, Latin, and German equivalents. In that work he translated the Hebrew word *togarmai as Türck* in German and *Turca* in Latin.

8. Sami Nadar, "Natural Gas Resources May be Backstory in Syria War," *Al-Monitor*, October 8, 2013.

9. "Israel Pitches 'Massive' Natural Gas Pipeline Plan to Europe," *Tim Times of Israel*, November 20, 2014. The report adds: "Israel has proposed that EU countries invest in a multi-billion euro pipeline to carry its natural gas to the continent, noting that the supply from Israel would reduce Europe's current dependence on natural gas from Russia."

Chapter 10: God's Battle Plan for Victory

1. Franklin D. Roosevelt, "Presidential Inaugural Address," March 4, 1933.

2. Martin Luther, "A Mighty Fortress Is Our God, verse 1. In public domain.

3. Personal interview, Mark Tobey with Daniel Miller, June 2014.

4. Wade Akins, *Sharing Your Faith with Muslims* (Garland, TX: Hannibal Books, 2011), 101.

5. Howard G. Hendricks, "Never Stop Growing," Founder's Week Message at Moody Bible Institute, February 1, 2005.

6. John F. Walvoord, *Revelation*, rev. and ed. by Philip E. Rawley and Mark Hitchcock (Chicago: Moody, 2011), 198.

Chapter 11: Staying Calm in Chaos

1. Leif Enger, *Peace Like a River* (New York: Grove Atlantic Press, 2001), 36.

2. David L. Akin, *10 Who Changed the World* (Nashville: Broadman & Holman, 2012), 81.

3. The New Testament repeats that promise in Hebrews 13:5 about providing our needs, so we need not be anxious, and Jesus promises His presence and comfort to all who trust in Him (see Matthew 28:20). In Matthew 11:28 Jesus promises to "all who are weary and heavy-laden . . . I will give you rest."

4. "How Firm a Foundation," verses 2, 4, 5, Rippon's *Selection of Hymns*, 1787. In public domain.